The Gospel According to Generation X

The Culture of Adolescent Belief

David K. Lewis

Carley H. Dodd

Darryl L. Tippens

CASA Advocate
Foster Care

Also by Lewis, Dodd and Tippens:

SHATTERING THE SILENCE
—Telling the Church the Truth About
Kids and Sexuality

DYING TO TELL
—The Hidden Meaning of
Adolescent Substance Abuse

Printed in the United States of America

ISBN **0-89112-015-7**

Library of Congress Card Number **94-74299** **1,2,3,4,5**

ACKNOWLEDGMENTS

A book of this sort is necessarily a community effort. It exists only because many different people were willing to support, encourage, and believe in our dream of helping families and congregations minister to adolescents. We cannot adequately thank all the people who assisted us, yet we must at least express our deep gratitude to some of those who have urged us on, given us advice, and kept us at the task for the last four years: Dr. Royce Money, President of Abilene Christian University; Dr. Ian Fair, Dean of the College of Biblical Studies; Roberta Brown, Beth Hall, Chris Heard, Robbie Robinson, Elaine Reynolds, and Chad Allred, whose countless hours of tabulating, typing, evaluating, and editing have earned both our amazement and thanks. We also applaud the many youth ministers, ministers, elderships, and local congregations who have so kindly supplied the data essential to our study. Above all, we appreciate three long-suffering spouses—Pam, Ada, and Anne—who believe so deeply in our mission and in us.

Contents

Preface

Two siblings grow up together. One is deeply committed to Christ and the other rejects him. You wonder why.

Two best friends attend the same Sunday school class and church camps, but two years after high school one dedicates her life to missions and the other turns against Christianity. How can this be?

Almost half (45%) of all teenagers raised in Churches of Christ end their affiliation sometime after high school graduation. What went wrong?

Whether or not you're a parent, you've probably asked the fundamental question, "Where does faith come from?" or "Why do some children become committed Christians and others not?" We believe there are several answers—in Scripture, in the wisdom of parents and church leaders, and, certainly, in our adolescents. All we have to do is ask. And that's what we've done in this book.

How Are Our Kids Doing?

To tell the truth, we didn't intend to write this book—not originally. When we started our research a decade ago, we were simply trying to answer some basic questions about the moral behavior of teenagers in Churches of Christ. Some people told us Christian teenagers were following the same worldly pursuits as their secular peers. "Most Christian teenagers are sexually active," some alarmists told us. "Our teenagers are doing drugs just like all the other kids at school," others asserted darkly. Were they right?

A decade ago, there was no empirical data to settle these questions, so we began a long journey to find out. Through a series of surveys and two books, we developed a moral profile of adolescents in Churches of Christ. We found some bad news, but plenty of good news. We also looked for information that went beyond behavior. What motivates ethical behavior? we wondered. We discovered that faith in God has a definitive effect on adolescent behavior. That discovery, in turn, led to the biggest question of all: *Why do some children have faith when others don't? What, in other words, are the conditions that encourage children to take God seriously?*

Over the last three years we have probed, questioned, analyzed, and debated the responses of 4,000 adolescents from Churches of Christ throughout the United States. In 1991 we examined teenagers' views of God. In 1992, we focused on their attitudes toward Jesus, and in 1993 we examined their understanding of the Holy Spirit. We searched their words for every hint, nuance, and answer—however slight. We found a great deal that contributes to an understanding of spiritual formation which we share in the following chapters.

Who Are the "Generation X-ers"?

We hasten to say we have no tidy formula to make your child a spiritual giant. As parents of teenagers ourselves, we're reminded every day that children are creatures of choice, often dazzled (like their parents) by a myriad of options in a postmodern, pluralist world. Many find it incredibly difficult to shield themselves from the icy stings of secularism which relentlessly assault them.

No one can guarantee our children will be spiritually mature at age 21, any more than one can guarantee they will be paragons of physical health at that age. What we can do is make sure the nutrients and conditions essential for spiritual growth are available to them. We plant and water, let us say, but God gives the increase.

One of our most urgent tasks is to understand this new generation. Busters, Generation X-ers, Thirteeners—whatever you call them—their interests and attitudes are remarkably diverse and, at times, downright baffling. One objective of this book is simply to help us understand this "unknown generation." Our first two chapters are a call to notice what our children think and believe. Only then are we prepared to act intelligently.

What Can We Do?

Christians need not submit passively to the "culture of disbelief" which envelops them.[1] Despite the radical, secular turn of contemporary society, parents still have enormous opportunities, especially in their children's younger years, to define the culture in which their children reside. Churches and their families can work together to construct and sustain a flourishing "culture of belief" despite the hostile society surrounding us. In fact, Christians all over our country are already doing it. More parents and church leaders need to join them.

This book is, indirectly, a report card on our churches. Collectively, our congregations invest millions of dollars and person-hours helping our children grow up in the faith. We instruct thousands of kids each week in Bible classes. We send our children to summer camps and mission points all over the globe. What is the effect of all these investments of time and energy? Do our teens acquire an authentic, growing faith? Many of them do. In the following chapters we offer some specific strategies for action.

The truth is, the basic nutrients of spirituality are known. For example, the practice of the spiritual disciplines, the presence of loving, supportive parents, and the availability of wise, adult mentors are common features in the lives of most spiritually maturing teens. We just need to recognize these and other similar factors. We need to hone them and encourage their wider application in families and youth programs. Therefore, the central purpose of this book is to introduce those things that help children grow in the knowledge of God. The days when we passively inherited a culture of belief are gone. *Today, we must actively, intentionally build a culture of belief.*

Is There Hope?

Christian parents today are an anxious lot. In a world where 135,000 classmates are reported to carry guns to school each day, parents wonder if their children even have a future. In such a dangerous world, parents naturally worry, "What about my child? Will she be faithful?" We must hope—and trust God—despite the dangers.

Faith building is a mysterious process. In Simone Weil's gifted terms, "the action of grace in our hearts is secret and silent."[2] Faith is ultimately God's gift to us. It's not something you can force on anyone, least of all on a typical American teenager. The New Testament paraphrase *The Message* expresses it like this: "Saving is all his idea, and all his work. All we do is trust him enough to let him do it. It's God's gift from start to finish! We don't play the major role . . . . God does the making and saving" (Ephesians 2:8-10). Yet Christian adults must do more than passively wait. Hope entails action. Paul goes on to say, "[God] creates each of us by Christ Jesus to join him in the work he does, the good work he has gotten ready for us to do, work we had better be doing." We offer this book as an encouragement to Christian parents and church leaders to accept the work God has ordained them to do.

Most of our children love God sincerely. They want to know him well and intimately. Our God-ordained mission is to participate with our children in building a culture of belief that introduces them to him and encourages them to deeper faith until Jesus comes.

David K. Lewis
Carley H. Dodd
Darryl L. Tippens

Abilene Christian University
January, 1995

---

[1] We are indebted to Stephen L. Carter for his insights into the secularizing of America. See *The Culture of Disbelief: How American Law and Politics Trivialize Religious Devotion* (New York: Basic Books, 1993).

[2] Simone Weil, *Waiting for God* (New York: Harper and Row, 1951) 50.

1

Who Are These Kids?

Whether you like it or not, we are the thing that will replace you. —*The Gen X Reader*

Everything I write or think about now seems, in the end, to veer toward the religious. I can't alter this and so I try to create from it. This wasn't something I ever expected to happen. I don't know what I ever really expected, but it certainly wasn't this. —Douglas Coupland, author of *Generation X*

For I desire steadfast love and not sacrifice, the knowledge of God rather than burnt offerings. —Hosea 6:6

Every generation worries about the next one coming along. That's the prescribed role of aging adults, it seems. Parents fear their children will squander the hard-won family treasures, whether material or spiritual. This almost universal anxiety about the young has reached a fever pitch after the media's frequent negative portrayals of the post-Baby Boomer generation (children born between 1965 and 1980), variously called the Baby Busters, "twentysomethings," "Thirteeners" (since they are the thirteenth generation since the founding of America), and "Generation X." They have been caricatured as soft, whining, cynical MTV addicts. With such bad press, no wonder Christian adults are worried. How will these sloppy slackers preserve the Gospel of Jesus Christ?

Is the media portrayal a stereotype smacking of tabloid journalism? How does one generalize about 38 million very diverse people? Parents shouldn't be overly concerned about such alarming generalizations. They're a combination of media myth and fact. Almost every generalization about the new generation demands qualification and revision. Some observers like Jane Bryant Quinn argue that they are not irresponsible, but rather more cautious and conservative than their parents.[1] Furthermore, we have to remind ourselves that what *may* be true about many Generation X-ers at large, may not necessarily hold true for Christian young adults. Our studies of Christian teens convince us that they are not generally self-pitying "slackers," indifferent to hard work or values. In many respects they are realists and, like their parents before them, impatient with the mistakes and questionable values of the previous generation.

While many news organizations and opinion polls have assessed the attitudes of the young, we think much has been left out—particularly their unique spirituality. For this reason, our assessment of Christian adolescents is an important set of data that will more fully indicate our children's spiritual future. And though our study focuses exclusively on adolescents in Churches of Christ, we strongly suspect this information is applicable to children from other evangelical traditions.

Are our children drifting from their parents' values? This is the big question to which adults want a definitive answer. The answer is yes. . . and no. The answer must be a bit ambiguous because everyone involved is "drifting." The evaluator usually overlooks the fact that he or she is in dynamic movement, as well as those being evaluated. Adults can easily see the next generation's shifting, but not their own. However, if we are all in flux, moving in the river of time, it's not entirely fair to pretend that one's own position is firmly fixed while criticizing everyone else's drift. If adults view themselves as having safely "arrived," then it's easy for them to wonder why their children should want to sail out of the comfortable harbor they have so generously provided. Perhaps a secondary benefit of this study will arise when adults turn to assess their own culture. It's very useful to understand what *generated* Generation X. One thing's for sure: the new generation came from somewhere—in fact, it came from us!

In many ways our children mirror us. Today's children will surely carry many—perhaps most—of their parents' core values into the next generation. On the other hand, it's also clear that in certain ways the faith of our children will have a decidedly different cast from our own. In this chapter we hope to define the continuity as well as the change in adolescent belief. And we hope to suggest some reasons for the changes. Finally, we conclude with some strategies for helping our children stay true to the Gospel of Jesus Christ.

In order to measure our childrens' spiritual orientation, we asked them to evaluate fifty statements asserting doctrinal and ethical positions held by members of the Churches of Christ in recent years. Statements ranged from foundational principles like, "Jesus is the divine Son of God" and "Jesus was raised from the dead" to controversial propositions such as, "The King James Version of the Bible is the only accurate version" and "Contemporary Christian music is sinful." We wanted to identify the propositions which elicited the greatest measure of agreement from our adolescents, as well as those which they would judge untrue or irrelevant. In order of descending agreement, this is what they told us:

- 97%—God loved the world so much that he gave his son to save the people from their sins.

- 97%—Jesus was raised from the dead.
- 96%—Jesus was the divine Son of God.
- 96%—Prayer is essential for anyone who wishes to grow spiritually.
- 95%—Jesus is coming back again from heaven to take his followers home.
- 95%—The devil actually exists today and is strongly influencing our world.
- 92%—Letting Jesus be Lord (ruler and king) is absolutely necessary for salvation.
- 90%—God has been and will always be involved in the affairs of this world.
- 88%—It would be extremely difficult, if not impossible, to make it in our world without the help of the Holy Spirit.
- 85%—God guided the authors of each of the books of the Bible as they wrote.
- 80%—It is still possible for Satan to enter into people today and take control of their lives.
- 76%—God will actually punish the wicked in a literal hell.
- 72%—Homosexuals have no chance for salvation unless they repent and change their life-style.
- 68%—The Lord's Supper must be taken on the first day of every week.
- 67%—Adultery is the only biblical reason for divorce.
- 61%—Every word of Scripture came directly from God.

- 60%—Evangelism is the most important work for the 20th-century church.
- 60%—Christians should be very different and distinctive from those in the world in dress, language and basic values of life.
- 59%—There must be elders and deacons in every church.
- 59%—All commandments in the Bible are of equal value and importance.
- 55%—It is impossible for any adult to be saved without being baptized.
- 49%—Abortion is strictly forbidden in the Bible, with no exceptions.
- 46%—Sunday is the most important day of any Christian's week.
- 44%—One could find salvation in many churches other than Churches of Christ.
- 42%—Every commandment in the New Testament must be literally obeyed.
- 40%—Christians must avoid any and all use of alcoholic beverages.
- 40%—Speaking in tongues is simply not scriptural.
- 39%—Christians should only marry Christians.
- 33%—One is not held responsible or accountable for his or her actions before becoming a Christian.
- 32%—In this decade, women should take much more of a leadership role than they have ever done before.

- 29%—What's taught in the Old Testament is very interesting and often important, but not essential for Christians today.
- 24%—Jesus should be taken very literally when he said that it's almost impossible for the rich to be saved.
- 23%—There is only one true church and that is the Church of Christ.
- 22%—Churches will not do well without a full-time preacher.
- 21%—It would be very important that Baptist and Christian folks be "re-baptized" before they are accepted into the fellowship of Churches of Christ.
- 20%—Divorce and remarriage for reasons other than adultery will cause all parties involved to be lost.
- 19%—Using musical instruments during a church service is sinful.
- 19%—Nations who do not hear the good news about Jesus have no hope of eternal life or salvation.
- 19%— "Church of Christ" is the only scriptural name for the church.
- 16%—Being a member of the Church of Christ is an absolute necessity for salvation.
- 13%—There is really little difference between Churches of Christ and denominations today.
- 13%—Meditation and fasting are two non-negotiable disciplines for the committed disciple.

- 13%—It is wrong to allow girls in youth devotionals to participate in praying and leading singing.
- 9%—All who are not members of the Church of Christ will be lost.
- 8%—Dancing in almost any form is always wrong for the Christian.
- 8%—One should never use instrumental music when singing about God, whether in church or out of church.
- 6%—The King James Version of the Bible is the only accurate version.
- 6%—Contemporary Christian music is sinful.
- 3%—Boys and girls swimming together is sinful.

The information in this table is striking, especially to anyone who knows the topics of debate that have raged within Churches of Christ for the last 50 years. On the one hand, nearly everyone can be encouraged by what our children *do* highly value. They appear to have accepted principles that nearly everyone would call the core message of the Gospel. Our young people agree with the Apostle Paul's principles "of first importance: That Christ died for our sins in accordance with the Scriptures, and that he was buried, and that he was raised on the third day in accordance with the Scriptures . . ." (1 Corinthians 15:3, NIV). Whatever else we conclude, we can be glad the majority of our teens believe in the saving power of Jesus Christ. They also believe in prayer. They take Satan seriously. Most accept adult immersion, weekly communion, and the inspiration of Scripture. We should not fear great numbers of our young people abandoning the core teachings of the Bible, based upon what they tell us.

Yet there is cause for concern. Some readers will find

certain cherished personal convictions far down the list from where they would like to see them. Obviously, some teens are not as distressed by adultery or abortion as their parents. Some teens are not eager to maintain the identifying markers of Churches of Christ. In general, we note that our youths (to varying degrees) reject those hallmarks of the Restoration tradition that distinguish us from other Christian groups. For example, the label "Church of Christ," the allowance of only vocal music in the assembly, the re-baptism of people from other churches—such items are optional matters to some (but certainly not all) adolescents within Churches of Christ.

That these items have become marginalized will distress many older Christians who see these as foundational, core concepts. "Why are our children selling out?" many will ask. This phenomenon of downplaying our institutional markers demands extensive comment. First, we will talk about the historical context for this rethinking of the "core Gospel." Second, we'll try to identify some of the social forces that are driving our young people to abandon the unique, identifying markers of Churches of Christ. Finally, we'll suggest some necessary responses.

Quest for the Core

We will better understand where our teens are headed if we take a moment to review our history. In attempting to prioritize what they have been taught in order to decide what to keep and what to discard, our children are continuing a process practiced throughout the centuries. Sometimes the process has resulted in modest change, sometimes in radical change, depending on the era. It happened in the Reformation. It happened in the early nineteenth century when the followers of Alexander Campbell and Barton Stone critiqued their Presbyterian heritage in order to rediscover the "ancient order." And it happened once again in the 1960's when many of today's church leaders re-examined their churches and found that they had not fully realized the Gospel in matters of social justice or vital worship. Every age must ask the question, "What is the core Gospel?"

In a sense, this question of the core goes back to the Old Testament when the prophets confronted Israel with the inconsistency of her faith and practice. Micah accused the people of his day of neglecting the core of faith: "And what does the Lord require of you but to do justice, and to love kindness, and to walk humbly with your God?" (6:8, NRSV). Hosea also declares a core theology when he urges his audience to practice heartfelt love for God: "For I desire steadfast love and not sacrifice, the knowledge of God rather than burnt offerings" (6:6, NRSV). In Jesus' day the debate over the core intensified. Nearly everyone (including the Pharisees and Jesus' disciples) concurred that not all commandments were of equal weight. There were "least" commandments (Matthew 5:19), and "weightier matters" like justice, mercy and faith (Matthew 23:23). While one should observe all of God's law, Jesus clearly taught that some parts of the law were simply more important. There is one great command that supersedes all the rest: love God with all your heart, soul, and mind (Matthew 22:37). Furthermore, many "laws" that had been bound by traditionalists, Jesus explained, were actually optional because they were only human traditions disguised as God's obligatory laws. Rules about Sabbath keeping and ritual cleansings are examples of teachings that were "core" for the Pharisees but which Jesus marginalized.

Much of Christian history has been marked by the human effort to settle the core. In Reformation England, for example, the Puritans wrestled intensely with this question. After all, how could Puritans effectively "purify" a church if they did not know what was core and what was not? The

Puritans articulated what they called "the doctrine of things indifferent." "Things indifferent" was their name for religious beliefs which people held personally, but which could not be bound upon others. That is, "things indifferent" could not be counted as core issues over which believers might divide. However, the Puritans became hopelessly divided in successive generations. After fighting the Anglicans, they turned on one another with ferocious zeal because they could not agree on "things indifferent."

In the Restoration movement, the sorting has continued on apace. "In matters of faith—unity. In matters of opinion—liberty. In all things—love" was the watch word and slogan. Yet no one succeeded in devising a universally acceptable list of the core elements, nor were we able to establish a universal method for separating faith matters (i.e., core) from opinions (i.e., "things indifferent").[2]

One point is clear, even though many Christians are reluctant to acknowledge it: nowhere in Scripture are we given a definitive list of the core teachings, though Jesus and Paul certainly enumerate some of the core items of our faith—justice, mercy, and faith (Matthew 23:23), love (1 Corinthians 13:13), and belief in Jesus' death and resurrection (1 Corinthians 15).

In view of this continuing struggle, should we be surprised that our own young people are trying to define the core? Aren't they really declaring to us that they are faithful sons and daughters of the Restoration Movement when they raise fundamental questions about what is core and what is not? Their searching and sifting are intrinsic to our religious movement.

We can question the methods our young people are using to make their decisions. We can look at their milieu and recognize the cultural influences that sway their thinking.

And we can ask tough questions about what is motivating the questioning: is it inspired by Scripture and the love of God, or is it driven by the desire to accommodate religion to environment?

Imitating Mom and Dad

When Dr. Royce Money, President of Abilene Christian University, looked at the statistics beginning on page 15, he observed, "These adolescents seem to reflect their parents' private views of God as opposed to the congregational or community views of God. Teenagers mirror what their parents privately believe." Money's insight is consistent with our knowledge of many Christian parents. The point is that young people do not mysteriously adopt a set of values *ex nihilo*, out of nothing. They come from somewhere and that somewhere includes the home. We suspect just what Dr. Money supposes: our teens are openly declaring ideas which their parents privately entertain. Their parents long ago decided what they believed about social issues like dancing and "mixed swimming." In various ways these parents implicitly or explicitly transmitted these values to their children. Though these parents would never publicly promote their point of view, they may have let their kids go to swimming parties or senior proms. The kids know what their parents believe on many topics, even if they were never formally discussed.

Consequently, we are slow to say that our children are "drifting" from parental values. Quite the opposite, they may be *embracing and enacting* them! We suspect a similar thing is happening with the demise of denominationally-distinctive markers. Today's parents are generally less sectarian (and more generally "evangelical" or "ecumenical") than their parents were. Once again, in the interest of congregational harmony, today's parents don't generally speak out on the matter. But their Generation X children, reading their parents' tolerant attitudes, are implementing the beliefs those attitudes imply.

On the other hand, not everything affecting our teens' attitudes comes from Mom and Dad. A great deal is coming from outside the home. Secular cultural forces, especially electronic media and popular culture, are exerting their own persuasive pressures. Some of the messages of our culture are good (respect for minorities, compassion for the poor, and others), but some directly threaten the Christian community. Others are ambiguous. The late Kurt Cobain, for example, through his rock albums attempted to convey a message of tolerance. In one famous incident Cobain became furious when he learned that two men who claimed to admire his music had raped a woman. On his next album, he included this message: "I have a request for our fans. If any of you hate homosexuals, people of different color, or women, please do this one thing for us—leave us [expletive] alone."[3]

A kind of sentimental, love-everyone, live-and-let-live mentality pervades much of pop culture. The one unforgivable sin in this culture is to "judge" another, to declare one's loyalty to one "-ism" over another. In the New Age gospel, everything is strictly equal and, preferably, private and individual—it's OK to be a Christian, but keep it to yourself. "Proselytizing" is not only illogical, it's arrogant and threatening to the homogenizing, syncretistic goal of the secular society. If our kids listen to the media (and how can they avoid it?), then they hear these themes daily. We should not be surprised if we see our teens love their church on the one hand, but feel reluctant to say that it is uniquely the church of God. Such exclusivism requires one to be extremely counter-cultural.

Teens hear much about human frailty and brokenness. *Generation X* author Douglas Coupland can say frankly, "I think I am a broken person."[4] The human need for a transcendent source of help makes good sense to teens who believe they live in a fallen, cock-eyed world. Yet, Christianity does not enjoy special status as the preferred spiritual option in the X-er supermarket of cosmic solutions. And in some areas of our culture, Christianity has even been moved to the back of the shelf or has been yanked from the shelf altogether.

Our adolescents live in an age of "choice." We choose our favorite brands of toothpaste, cars, clothing, music, and even lifestyles. Why not morality, ethics, and religious beliefs? All principles become preferences. In a recent Barna poll, 70% of X-ers said there was no such thing as absolute truth.[5] Not all our Christian young people subscribe to the spirit of this age, but we must realistically acknowledge the uphill struggle to maintain a religious faith that asserts its objectivity, absolute truth, and uniqueness in the marketplace of religious ideologies and competing philosophies.

In the Boat Together

We must understand that Christian youths often feel assaulted by a chorus of hostile secular and non-Christian voices. This explains why they huddle with evangelical believers—from various denominations—at work, at school, and on the playing field. The hostility of the popular culture inevitably causes our youth to overlook the historic doctrinal differences between themselves and other Christian believers.

The American writer Stephen Crane tells of being lost at sea in a small boat after his ship capsized off the coast of Florida. For two days he shared the tiny boat with the captain and two other strangers. The sea was extremely rough, and for about 40 hours they were in constant danger of drowning. In the life-threatening crisis, these perfect strangers pulled together, and they felt a profound sense of brotherhood: "No one mentioned it. But it dwelt in the boat, and each man felt it warm him. They were a captain, an oiler, a cook, and a correspondent, and they were friends, friends in a more curiously iron-bound degree than may be common."[6] Teenagers from conservative churches face a hostile sea of opposition. Some feel that they are about to be swamped by waves of secularism, hedonism, and moral relativism. Like Stephen Crane's companions in a violent sea, our youth feel a comradeship and friendship with other evangelicals. They help each other survive. They support and care for one another. To change metaphors: seeing themselves in the war zone, our youth don't recognize the need for arcane theological disputes. In view of their daily battles with a secular world (Does God exist? Is Christianity true?), some of our old doctrinal disputes seem incomprehensible. They sense that believers in Christ have more uniting them than separating them. We are in the same boat, they think. They sing: "Stop the fighting and start uniting."[7]

The trend to accept fellow believers not only derives from personal friendships forged in a hostile dominant culture. The spirit of acceptance also comes from an evangelical subculture which teens experience in a variety of ways. As the dominant secular culture becomes ever more unfriendly to Christians, Christian groups find more common ground among themselves, and the boundaries between Christian groups become more permeable. We are more willing to hear what others have to say. Thus, kids growing up in Churches of Christ, like their parents, have easy access to the ideas of C. S. Lewis, Billy Graham, James Dobson, Chuck Colson, Tony Campolo, and dozens of others. Contemporary Christian music is especially persuasive, as well. Evangelical ideas are also available through books, tapes, CD's, radio, television and countless evangelical organizations like the Fellowship of Christian Athletes.

Finally, the impetus to celebrate common ground among Christian believers rather than fighting one another is coming from within the Churches of Christ. No doubt, some of today's preaching encourages this. In addition, some of the most popular new hymns convey the message of unity. Since the 1960's, hymns like Peter Scholtes's "We Are One in the Spirit" have fostered a spirit of respect and cooperation:

> We are one in the Spirit, we are one in the Lord,
> We are one in the Spirit, we are one in the Lord,
> And we pray that our unity may one day be restored:
> And they'll know we are Christians by our love, by our love,
> And they'll know we are Christians by our love.

Though the "we" is ambiguous in this hymn, many young Christians obviously mean to include more than those people who happen to be attending their local congregation. From all directions—parents, secular culture, evangelical subculture, and their congregations—our young people have been asked to downplay sectarian loyalty. They have gotten the message.

Danger Points

As we mentioned at the outset, in the process of re-evaluating the core of the Gospel, our children will make their own choices—some good, some bad. The search is inherently good because it is only through their personal struggle that the faith will become truly their own. Faith is not inherited. It is earned. Or, rather, it is born in the midst of personal struggle. We see this happening.

Yet, we recognize real dangers, too. We are disturbed that our young people are in danger of embracing a faith contaminated by the present age (a danger in every generation). We see a tendency to compromise on major ethical questions like sexual morality and abortion. We have a right to wonder if our children's faith will be hobbled by the idols of popular culture.

We can't make ultimate faith decisions for our children, but there is plenty we can do. First, we can clarify our own theology. Surely, some of our children's confusion is a reflection of their parents' unfocused faith system. It's high time we clearly articulated what we believe the Bible teaches about God, Christ, the Holy Spirit, the church, the nature of humanity, sin, redemption and "the last things" (i.e., heaven, hell, and the last judgment). There is ample evidence that many conservative and evangelical churches are abandoning their historic theological views.[8] We must look within and conduct our own spiritual inventory. A serious and extensive study of the Bible should occur in all our congregations and in all our families. If they are going to establish any sense of the "core" of the faith for themselves, our children need to know, unequivocally, what we believe.

But there is more to be done. We must be in such relationships with our children that we can hear them, understand them, and share in their faith struggles. Prepackaged answers delivered to people who are in pain seldom achieve their intended purpose. Because the business of living is too complicated, individual and anguishing, we cannot just drop a systematic theology into our children's laps and expect a magical transformation. Instead, we have to listen to their particular formulations of the eternal questions: Who am I? Where have I come from? Where am I going? And then we need to help them discover for themselves the answers to these questions. In Henri Nouwen's terms, we have to allow them to "live the questions."

While granting them permission to ask the questions, we must model Jesus' life to them. We must show them daily what it means to imitate Christ. In other words, we don't hand them a theology to read—we join them on a life-changing journey. We connect with them so intimately that they become our spiritual apprentices. This was Paul's method for developing faith in Timothy:

> Now you have observed my teaching, my conduct, my aim in life, my faith, my patience, my love, my steadfastness, my persecutions and suffering . . . continue in what you have learned and firmly believed, knowing from whom you have learned it . . . (2 Timothy 3:10,14, NRSV)

Paul closely links doctrinal instruction and mentoring. Together they compose a seamless pedagogical method. We must return to *apprenticeship* Christianity. It's the only kind that works.

In other words, we are calling for a reunion of theology and spirituality—the study of the truths about God and the exemplary life of faith that will give power and meaning to it all. This will require a new appreciation for the family of God, to be examined more fully in the following chapters.

---

[1] Jane Bryant Quinn, "The Luck of the Xers," *Newsweek* 6 June 1994: 67.

[2] In recent works like Bill Love's *The Core Gospel* we see the continuing relevance of this struggle to our tradition. See Bill Love, *The Core Gospel: On Restoring the Crux of the Matter* (Abilene: ACU Press, 1992).

[3] Qtd. in Jeff Giles, "The Poet of Alienation," *Newsweek* 18 April 1994: 47.

[4] Qtd. in Andrés Tapia, "Reaching the First Post-Christian Generation," *Christianity Today* 12 Sept. 1994: 23.

[5] George Barna, *The Invisible Generation: Baby Busters* (Glendale, CA: Barna Research group, 1992) 81.

[6] "The Open Boat," *The Portable Stephen Crane* Ed. Joseph Katz (New York: Viking Press, 1969) 365.

[7] Acappella, "Let's Get Together," *Better Than Life*, n.d.

[8] See, for example, Martin Marty, *The Great Schism: Three Paths to the Secular* (New York: Harper & Row, 1969); David F. Wells, *No Place for Truth: Whatever Happened to Evangelical Theology?* (Grand Rapids: Eerdmans, 1993); Robert Wuthnow, *The Struggle for America's Soul: Evangelicals, Liberals, and Secularism* (Grand Rapids: Eerdmans, 1989) and *The Restructuring of American Religion: Society and Faith since World War II* (Princeton: Princeton UP, 1988).

2

WHO IS THEIR GOD?

When Christ calls a man, he bids him come and die.
—Dietrich Bonhoeffer

"But who do you say that I am?" Peter answered, "The Messiah of God." —Luke 9:20

The way any particular age has depicted Jesus is often a key to the genius of that age. —Jaroslav Pelikan

---

One way of understanding a generation's spiritual life is to examine its views of God. Our teens willingly shared with us their personal impressions of God, Christ, and the Holy Spirit. We found this large collection of personal theologies riveting and insightful, both because of what our respondents included and because of what they conspicuously left out. On the whole, our teens' theological views are deeply rooted in the scriptural tradition, yet we are puzzled that certain traits of God's character, fundamental in Scripture, tend to be minimized or even rejected by some of today's teens. We must ask, "Why is this so?"

Jaroslav Pelikan, the eminent church historian, explains in *Jesus Through the Centuries* that each generation must come to terms with the meaning of Jesus of Nazareth.[1] Every generation of Christians attempts to realize the meaning of God the Father, Christ, and the Holy Spirit through an array of vivid metaphors and analogies. The Bible is, in fact, a giant gallery of metaphoric descriptions of the deity. He is variously king, judge, father, brother, mother, friend, rock, dove, fire, wind, shepherd, lamb, word, bridegroom, lover, master, warrior, bread, water, wine, light. . . and the list goes on. While all these images are available through Scripture, not all of them communicate with equal force to every age, culture, or social group.

Pelikan, for example, shows that each historical epoch responds most passionately to a particular image of Jesus Christ, selected from the vast menu of available pictures, often ignoring other, less congenial, images. To the earliest Jewish Christians, Jesus was the master teacher, the great Rabbi. To Platonist believers Jesus was the Logos, the Divine Reason. Travel to the Archiepiscopal Chapel in Ravenna, Italy, and look at the sixth century mosaic of Christ as "Christus Victor." Christ stares forward boldly, almost defiantly. He looms above in full battle dress, one foot poised on the head of a crushed serpent, another pressing down on the head of lion. A small cross is balanced on his right shoulder, clearly suggesting a warrior's battle sword, not an instrument of torture. In that age and time, believers saw in Jesus their conquering hero. By contrast, in our own day, many of our readers would be uncomfortable with the militant Christ of Ravenna. We are more at home with the gentle Good Shepherd who tenderly retrieves lost lambs from the world's thickets.

The point is this: no single age or generation exclusively owns, controls, or manages the mental pictures of Father, Christ, or the Holy Spirit. For God to be understood, appreciated, and taken seriously, he must somehow be communicated in terms that make sense to each culture. At the same time, each culture must be called to seek faithfully the true God of Scripture. Each age and generation must not be allowed merely to pick and choose the images of God that are congenial. However demanding the quest, realizing the richness, depth, complexity, and otherness of God's nature must be our goal.

We believe the images of Father, Christ, and Holy Spirit current among our children are profoundly indicative of their spiritual lives. According to Pelikan, "It has been characteristic of each age of history to depict Jesus in accordance with its own character."[2] Each generation, in other words, comes to Scripture to find God; but each generation brings something (needs, beliefs, longings, expectations) to the search. Through our teenagers' chosen metaphors for the Trinity, we are able to peer into their most deeply held attitudes and convictions. We believe our teens' perceptions of God reveal their own "theologies." We also believe the particular attitudes about God (implied through their positive and negative images of him) reveal the degree to which our teenagers are willing to live morally and spiritually committed lives. In other words, we think the images our kids have of God actually compose the *very foundation of their ethical and moral behavior.* Tell us how your children imagine God, and we will tell you something of how they will act in a crisis or a dilemma.

Taking note of our children's conceptions of God has other benefits as well. Our children's perceptions of God serve as a kind of report card on the religious education they have received from their parents and church leaders. Their conceptions of God reveal whether we have been successful in instilling a truly biblical theology in the hearts of our children. Finally, we believe this assessment of our children's understandings of God should cause adults to conduct a personal spiritual inventory. It is altogether possible that we, the parents and church leaders, are responsible for transmitting inadequate and incomplete understandings of God to our children, precisely because our own understandings of God are inadequate and incomplete.

How Teens View God the Father—Compassionate Friend

Most teens attending our churches tell us that they take God the Father very seriously (85%); tragically, however, 15% indicate that they are either on the verge of abandoning faith or have already rejected God. What is causing some to hold fast to God, while others are moving away from the Lord and Creator? The answers are complex, but one important element concerns their view of him. Our children, in fact, hold radically variant opinions about God, and these opinions are closely related to such matters as personal spiritual loyalty and ethical living. Some view God in a positive way (as patient, forgiving, warm, loving) which causes them to feel deep loyalty to him. Others view him so negatively (as critical, harsh, demanding) that they are in danger of rejecting him. Our teens attribute a number of qualities to God. For example:

- 93% say God is p*atient* with me
- 93% say God is *forgiving* of me
- 92% say God can be *counted on*
- 92% say God is *interested* in me
- 92% say God takes me *seriously*
- 92% say God is *warm* and *loving*
- 83% say God is easy to get *close* to
- 44% say God tends to be *critical*
- 40% say God is *lighthearted* and *playful*

- 12% say God is *harsh* and *demanding*
- 11% say God is *angry*

Overwhelmingly, our youth find God to be loving, compassionate, and approachable. Since our respondents are largely members of the family of God, we aren't surprised that they hold these positive attitudes about their Creator.[3] Their positive feelings about the Father are consistent with much of Scripture, which portrays the Creator as merciful and compassionate. Our children hold a view closely resembling that of the Psalmist:

> The Lord is merciful and gracious,
> Slow to anger and abounding in steadfast love. . . .
> He does not deal with us according to our sins,
> Nor repay us according to our iniquities.
> For as the heavens are high above the earth,
> So great is his steadfast love
> Toward those who fear him;
> As far as the east is from the west,
> So far he removes our transgressions from us.
> As a father has compassion for his children,
> So the Lord has compassion for those who fear him.
> For he knows how we were made;
> He remembers that we are dust. (103:8-14, NRSV)

Our young people have generally accepted this God of compassion and grace. The father in Jesus' story of the prodigal son is perhaps the closest approximation to our children's preferred image. Later in this chapter we'll raise questions about the benefits and the dangers that may be hidden in this preferred image of the heavenly Father. But first, let's consider teens' images of Jesus Christ and the Holy Spirit.

How Teens View Christ—Friend and Guide

Every parent, minister, and youth worker dreams of the day the children in their charge will not only know God, but will also come to love his Son and submit to his rule in their lives. We know our influence over our children is finite and time-bound. The day comes only too soon when each child must stand on his or her own feet and decide the direction for life. Christ's reign can only begin when a person chooses obedience to the King's rule. How well is today's church raising its children to be responsive to the call to discipleship? What is our children's concept of Christ? Figure 2.1 exhibits the major metaphors which our children hold about Jesus Christ.

PICTURES OF CHRIST

(+)

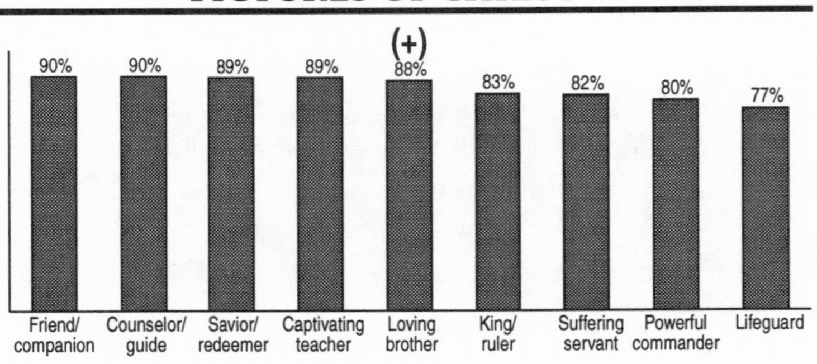

(-)

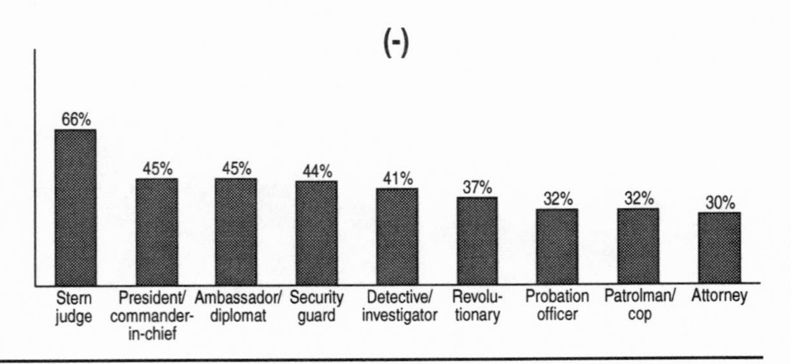

FIGURE 2.1

Similar to their view of God the Father, our teens have overwhelmingly positive views of Jesus. As the two graphs in Figure 2.1 indicate, 90% see Jesus as a friend, companion, counselor, or guide. Other positive designations receive high marks as well: Jesus is savior, redeemer, loving brother, king, suffering servant, commander, and even lifeguard. The images are not always "soft" and easy-going, however. Two-thirds recognize him as a demanding judge, yet they largely reject a Jesus who might be designated detective, revolutionary, cop, or attorney. Why? Partly because this last set of labels generally falls outside the scope of biblical language or categories. But also, we think, because they suggest a Lord who is demanding, coercive, and negative. For many of our children, Jesus could never be seen as a hard-nosed critic.

Despite these positive views of Christ, we found discouraging results when we looked at how closely our teens are actually following Christ. Over 20% of our teens state that they "rarely, if ever" ask the question, "What would Jesus do in this situation?" Only 28% report they willingly and naturally turn to Jesus for assistance for daily problems. The remaining teens are somewhere in the middle, occasionally consulting Scripture and the Lord about the difficult decisions in their lives.

We were a bit more encouraged when we asked, "In which areas of your life does Christ make a difference?" Here are the results:

- 91% see Christ as very important in their future.
- 87% see the church as very important in their future.
- 85% declare Jesus affects their personal involvement in church.
- 71% indicate Christ influences their use (or non-use) of alcohol.

- Approximately 66% claim Christ makes a difference in choosing friends, sexual behavior, and decisions about cheating at school.
- 60% report submitting their choice of colleges and dating partners to the Lord.

Yet even our excitement about these figures is tempered by the fact that many teens consider Christ less relevant in some parts of their lives. Less than half of the teens report that Jesus makes a difference in vocational choices, music preferences, use of leisure time, movie choices, and use of finances.

We wondered: Is there a relationship between the portrait a teenager holds of Jesus and his ethics? In fact, we think a person's mental picture of Christ is related to the degree of commitment one feels toward the acceptance of Christ's lordship in daily living. When we placed the images of Jesus alongside other predictors of lordship in daily life, the result proved to be startling. Teens who embraced the top nine views of Jesus (labeled with a plus sign in figure 2.1) were 28% *more likely to embrace Christian ethical principles* than those who held to the harsher images of Christ (labeled with a minus sign in figure 2.1). Among a number of variables which predict the acceptance of Christ's lordship in daily living, a teen's perception of Christ is the fourth most powerful predictor of ethical commitment.

Apparently, when negative views of Christ predominate, motivation to live for God weakens. This seems consistent with Paul's view that love, not law, is the best motivation for holy living. "The very spring of our actions is the love of Christ," Paul tells us in 2 Corinthians 5:14 (Phillips). "Through love become slaves of one another. For the whole law is summed up in a single commandment, 'You shall love your neighbor as yourself'" (Galatians 5:14, NRSV). Our teens' views of Christ are more than a statistical curiosity or a topic for academic discussion. These deeply held conceptions of Christ shape spiritual destinies. A clear, biblical, and positive image of the Lord can make a difference in everyday life. Those who lack a positive view of Christ are more likely to separate from him and follow their own inclinations.

On the other hand, we have every right to wonder if our teenagers have a full and complete grasp of the character of Jesus Christ. Is the friendly and loving Jesus the only Jesus they need to know? Are there other important features of the divine character which need to be added to our teens' repertoire of images? For example, what about Christ's judgment against the Pharisees' legalism or Peter's vacillation? What about his militant leadership in Revelation 1:1-16 and 2:12? Later in this chapter we'll return to the question of the biblical images of Christ that tend to be undervalued by today's teens.

How Teens View the Holy Spirit— The Great Encourager

Most of our teens view the Holy Spirit as active and constantly working in their lives and in the lives of the church. In light of the historic reluctance in the Restoration Movement to assign the Spirit an overt role in the church, we found this activist view somewhat surprising. Table 2.1 shows a number of activities our teens assign to the Holy Spirit.

Most of our teens see the Holy Spirit as the Great Encourager. Most (over 75%) reject the traditionally charismatic works of the Holy Spirit (healing, tongue-speaking, miraculous prophecy). Our teens are not always clear on how the Holy Spirit works since they usually respond in the middle range of the scale to questions about his nature, methods, power, focus, and involvement in our daily lives.

However, our teens firmly assert that the Spirit is important to the life of the Christian.

SENIOR HIGH TEENS' BELIEFS ABOUT THE HOLY SPIRIT'S WORK

The Holy Spirit . . .	*Priority Ranking*
• reassures me that I am a child of God when I begin to doubt	93%
• guarantees me that I will have eternal life now and forever	92%
• pours the love of God into my heart	91%
• is my own personal counselor who lives within me	90%
• interprets my heart to God when I don't have the words to express	89%
• gives me the power to confess verbally that Jesus is Lord	82%
• gives me special gifts (like wisdom, faith, mercy, & knowledge) to encourage and build up the church	80%
• gives me the power to avoid sexual immorality	77%
• appoints preachers/ministers and enables them to carry out their functions within the local church	76%
• keeps me from having a divisive and quarrelsome spirit	71%
• makes available to me the same power that raised Jesus from the dead	69%
• convicts me of sin by making me feel guilty	68%
• is able to know the inner thoughts of God and shares them with me	64%
• causes me to behave in such a way that at times others think I'm crazy or strange	30%
• enables me to do miraculous things such as healing, casting out demons, and/or other miraculous signs and wonders through the name of the Holy Spirit	24%
• enables me to speak in tongues, prophesy, and/or distinguish between the spirits	23%

TABLE 2.1

Teens' views also closely mirror their local congregation's teachings on the subject. Through a series of questions, we were able to ascertain the teens' home congregations' views about the Holy Spirit. We compared the teens who belong to churches which teach "non-direct" working by the Holy Spirit with teens of congregations teaching that the Spirit's work is direct. The first kind of church we label left-brain or rationalist churches; the latter we designate right-brain or affective churches. These two types are contrasted in Figure 2.2.

PERCEIVED IMPORTANCE OF THE HOLY SPIRIT FOR TEENS IN "RIGHT BRAIN" AND "LEFT BRAIN" CHURCHES

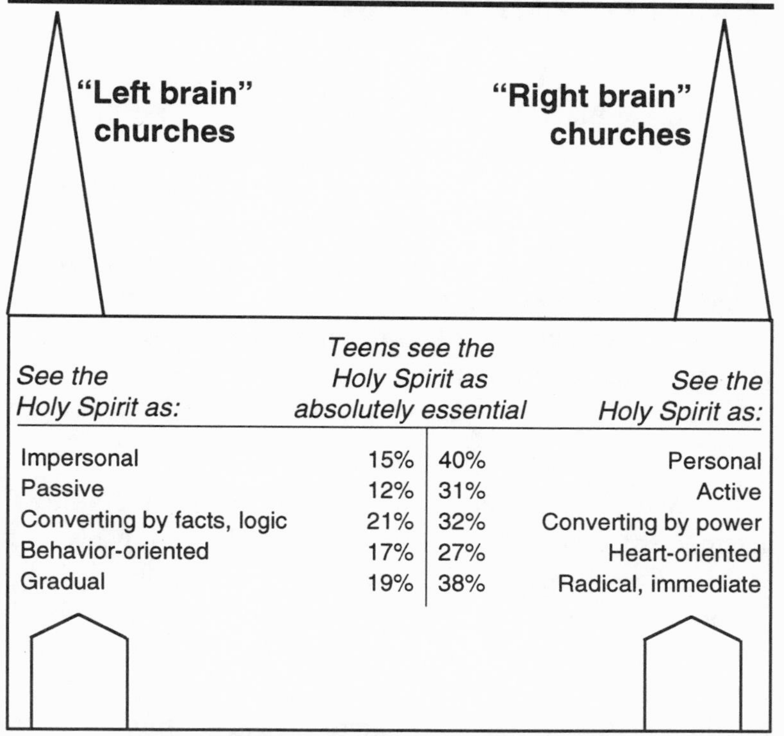

See the Holy Spirit as:	*Teens see the Holy Spirit as absolutely essential*		*See the Holy Spirit as:*
Impersonal	15%	40%	Personal
Passive	12%	31%	Active
Converting by facts, logic	21%	32%	Converting by power
Behavior-oriented	17%	27%	Heart-oriented
Gradual	19%	38%	Radical, immediate

- "Right brain" churches have teens with an average of one to two times greater likelihood of seeing the Holy Spirit as absolutely essential.

FIGURE 2.2

At the very least, we can say our teens closely mirror the teaching of their parent congregations on matters related to the Holy Spirit. And we can say that teens tend to take the Holy Spirit more seriously if they worship in congregations which teach and model a doctrine of the Holy Spirit's active role in today's world. Figure 2.2 indicates that teens from the right-brained churches—those which portray the Holy Spirit as personal, active, heart-oriented, radical, and powerful—are, on average, *one to two times more likely* to say the Spirit is essential than teens from churches which do not emphasize the Spirit's active mission in the life of the church.

The Controlling Metaphor—A User-Friendly Deity?

When we look collectively at our teens' images of God, we see much that is encouraging. The vast majority look upon him in wholesome and encouraging terms. The object of their worship is personal and active, compassionate and caring, involved and loving, friendly and close-at-hand. For most, God is the compassionate Father in heaven; Jesus is the Lord of their hearts, and the Spirit is a personal, indwelling Power. All of these primary images are biblical, and they appear to produce young adults who feel loyalty, commitment, and ethical responsibility. Could we ask for more?

We don't object to these controlling metaphors inasmuch as they are rooted in Scripture. Indeed, we adults can feel some pride knowing we've succeeded in teaching these very images to our children. Our children have absorbed the content of our teaching to a high degree. Yet we must register our concern. We recall Jaroslav Pelikan's point: "The way any particular age has depicted Jesus is often a key to the genius of that age."[4] We would paraphrase by saying that the way our children depict the Father, the Son, and the Holy Spirit is a significant key to the character of the new, post-boomer generation.

We note in particular that our children's deep need for a compassionate God is certainly biblical in origin. But will this God be so absolutely compassionate that "tough love" ceases to be a trait? It's one thing to see God as loving parent, quite another to make him indulgent to the point of dysfunction. C. S. Lewis noted this trend in English and American churches decades ago when he wryly observed that many of us don't want a Father in Heaven; rather, we want a Grandfather in Heaven, a benevolent and overly-indulgent benefactor who gives us what we want. We are not suggesting all our children have moved to this sentimental position—far from it. We recall that a full two-thirds of our youth also view God as a judge. However, because our children live in a secular culture, they have constant contact with an environment which encourages them to refashion their God into a kind of Cosmic Pacifier, the eternal dispenser of goodies, pats on the back, and friendly smiles. In short, they are being lured to invent a user-friendly deity, a "nice" God who affirms them and makes them feel good about themselves, no matter what.

We have to ask the tough question: are there attributes and word pictures of our God in Scripture which seem to be overlooked or minimized in any way? The answer is yes. What we find often being omitted from the menu of divine qualities is his transcendent power, his exclusive claims on us, his fierce judgment on evil and evil-doers, and his high demands for personal sacrifice. Earlier, we cited Psalm 103 as a fitting summation of the young Christian's view of God: "The Lord is merciful and gracious, slow to anger and abounding in steadfast love." But we purposefully deleted verse nine: "He will not always accuse, nor will he keep his anger forever." This stark picture of an angry, accusatory deity is much harder for young adults to take, yet it is woven seamlessly into a Psalm extolling God's abundant and steadfast love.

Few of the images of God most popular and accessible to our youth suggest a high-demand deity—one who calls us to sell all we have and die to self. Clearly, some of our adolescents have difficulty imagining a God who would tell anyone they are wrong about anything or that they might not make it to Heaven. Many young adults want an inclusive, "live-and-let-live" God, one ecumenical enough that just about anyone could fit into the divine household. Thus, children mirror this relativistic, multicultural, equal-opportunity age. On the one hand, they accept an array of metaphors portraying God as loving friend and parent. But this loving friend and parent is of a certain sort. He seldom, if ever, judges anyone.

This attitude emerged with shocking clarity when we asked teens what they would recommend a congregation do if it had members who were violating explicit teachings of the Bible. Should a congregation withdraw fellowship from them? And if so, for what reason? Significantly, nearly one-fourth of our respondents refused to address the question at all. Another quarter stated emphatically that no one should ever be withdrawn from, whatever the sin. While most felt very uncomfortable with the congregation taking disciplinary action against the sinful brother or sister, those who were comfortable with this process stated that fellowship should be withdrawn for the reasons listed in Table 2.2.

While our teens often have strong personal opinions about these issues, fewer than one percent of those surveyed believe that abortionists, blasphemers against the Holy Spirit, power-hungry elders, mate-swappers, or drug users should be removed from the fellowship. They express a surprising tolerance of offenders, apparently on the grounds that no one is to be "judged" by another. This attitude may be one more reflection of the privatization of faith. This attitude seems to go hand-in-hand with the concept of a non-judgmental, ever-forgiving God.

WHAT TEENS BELIEVE MERITS WITHDRAWAL OF FELLOWSHIP

When teens were asked about the issue of "withdrawing fellowship" from others within Churches of Christ, 22% refused to address the question at all; 14% stated up-front that they believed that no one should ever be "withdrawn from." Their belief was simply that God and not man should be the judge.

The following were issues that some of our teens believed merited removal from our fellowship. They are listed in priority order.

1 **An unrepentant heart demonstrated by continual sins** was considered reason for withdrawal of fellowship by some of our teens. 22% specifically mentioned adultery, 17% mentioned homosexuality, and 13% mentioned fornication.
2 **Divorce and remarriage for reasons other than adultery** was considered reason for withdrawal of fellowship by some of our teens.
3 **Teaching principles that clearly violated the core of the gospel** (Jesus' death, burial and resurrection) was considered reason for withdrawal of fellowship by some of our teens.
4 **Teaching a doctrine that cannot be tolerated by the elders of the church, and refusal to cease teaching the doctrine after confrontation** was considered reason for withdrawal of fellowship by some of our teens.
5 **Becoming involved in the occult or practicing Satanism** was considered reason for withdrawal of fellowship by some of our teens.
6 **Deviant sexual behaviors** (rape, incest and bestiality) were considered reason for withdrawal of fellowship by some of our teens.
7 **Causing division within churches of Christ** was considered reason for withdrawal of fellowship by some of our teens.
8 **Miscellaneous practices and beliefs:** practicing or condoning abortion, involvement with drugs or alcohol, refusing to attend services regularly, believing that miracles are possible today, insisting that women preach today, blaspheming the Holy Spirit, being power hungry within churches, involvement in mate swapping, advocating the Boston Movement and having a negative influence upon young children were mentioned by only 1% of the teens surveyed.

TABLE 2.2

What seems to be missing is the notion of a God who can be both lover *and* judge, compassionate *and* just, forgiving parent *and* demanding master. We suppose many of our teens would have trouble reconciling their view of God with many scriptural texts. What would they say about John the Baptist's harsh words to the crowds? "You brood of vipers! Who warned you to flee the wrath to come? Bear fruits worthy of repentance" (Luke 3:7, NRSV). They would apparently have trouble with Jesus' condemnation of the scribes and the Pharisees:

> But woe to you, scribes and Pharisees, hypocrites! For you lock people out of the kingdom of heaven. For you do not go in yourselves, and when others are going in, you stop them. Woe to you, scribes and Pharisees, hypocrites! For you cross sea and land to make a single convert, and you make the new convert twice as much a child of Hell as yourselves (Matthew 25:13-15, NRSV).

There is much in the Bible—both Old Testament and New—that does not square with a soft, user-friendly deity. Reverence, awe, and fear for a God who is "a consuming fire" (Hebrews 12:29) must be restored to the library of images used by our young people.

A Question of Balance

We assert that our teens need not—*must* not—abandon their positive images of God. In fact, we urge parents and church leaders to continue promoting positive conceptions of God. We state once again that when God is seen as warm, personally interested, forgiving, trustworthy, and patient, the majority of our kids (more than 80%) see God as "very important," and tell us they take him very seriously. Since these positive traits are fundamental characteristics of God in Scripture, and since belief in these traits apparently leads to faithful living, we certainly don't want to detract from this gracious view of God. We think the loving father of the prodigal, ready to forgive and forget, should be a foundational picture for Christians (Luke 15). But we must ask, "What features other than forgiveness are a part of God's character?" Can a parent be infinitely loving and also hold high expectations of his children? We should be able to take the positive images of God held by our children and supply additional details in his character—including our Father's demand for us to be perfect as he is perfect (Matthew 5:48). We must lead our children to understand that a gracious Father does not keep a wayward child in the household, no matter what. Separation and abandonment because of our own rebellion are clear possibilities.

We must be willing to introduce our children to all the elements of God's character, even when they go against the grain of today's culture. We must teach them that it is idolatry to worship their own desires, to try to make God be just what they want. We must teach that, because the God of Scripture stands above and beyond culture, he never quite fits our culture's expectations, needs, and wants.

Without abandoning the familiar and comforting qualities of God's character, it is our goal to stretch toward the unfamiliar, the counter-cultural, and the "scandalous" qualities of God's nature. No doubt, this would include the discovery of his exclusivity, his transcendence, and his unyielding judgment against evil. Starting with the two-dimensional deity they have known, we should lead them to the more balanced, comprehensive, and multi-dimensional view of God that characterizes spiritual maturity. We are talking about the right balance between many competing and complementary metaphors and traits. God is at once love and justice, the forgiver and the punisher, the safe haven and the consuming fire.

Parents and church leaders are not qualified to critique their children's distorted images of God until they have made sure their own standard, the template against which they judge others, is deeply rooted in biblical theology. We must admit that too many youth ministers (and the college curricula that educated them) have been theologically inadequate—big on function, shallow in content. We must redouble our commitment to ground all our teachers in the knowledge of God.

Three Metaphors for God

One of our immediate tasks is to come up with fuller portraits of God, based on Scripture. Dr. Leonard Allen, Professor of Bible at Abilene Christian University, offers an excellent place to begin this process.[5] He maintains that the Bible portrays three dominant pictures or controlling metaphors of God. One is the "Exodus God," revealed principally in Moses's leading Israel out of captivity. The picture emphasizes God's liberating power, setting humans free from bondage.

Second is the "Covenant-Making God." Through Abraham, David, the Prophets and others, God promises to be faithful to Israel. His love and mercy were first pledged to Abraham, but the promise extends to Israel and the church, the New Israel. This promise is reignited in the prophetic literature and is vividly portrayed in the metaphor of Israel as God's beloved bride.

Third, God is the "Grieving Parent." He hears the cries of the people when they are distressed, and he acts on their behalf because he shares their pain. For example, Isaiah speaks of God's compassion as being like that of a mother for her beloved children (Isaiah 66:12-13). This portrait of the Grieving Parent is powerfully fleshed out by Jesus in his parable of the two lost sons in Luke 15. There, God is not only the grieving parent; he is also the compassionate, seeking parent who wills the return of all his children, though he never coerces them or manipulates their freedom. Though the Father's love is infinite, the wayward child must choose to come home. A rebellious child can successfully resist even infinite parental love.

We believe these portraits of God will make sense to today's teens. Our children are in jeopardy if we leave them to patch together their own images of God drawn randomly from scraps of occasional Bible reading, sermons, hearsay, and contemporary Christian music. Allen warns us:

> Out of our ignorance and our pride, we form God in our own image. We make God a projection of what we want him to be, or what our culture says he is. We make God reflect our values, our psychology . . . The biblical word for this dynamic is idolatry. God becomes the projection of human wants and wishes.

Allen criticizes every generation, not just the newest one, for borrowing its gods from the spirit of the age. He speaks prophetically to us and our forebears: "And so, if you are a frontier people, your God possesses frontier values. If you are an affluent people, then your God sanctions affluence. If you are a warring people, your God sanctions war." Allen cautions all of us to look closely to see if our concepts of God are contaminated by the secular ideologies of the surrounding culture. The challenge is to own up to the pervasive human tendency (our tendency!) to make God into our own image. Allen calls us to resist this tendency, to return again to Scripture, and to rediscover the God of Scripture in all his depth, majesty, and glory.

When we do this, we will know the God our children must also know—the Faithful One who hears our deepest cries and holds us in his arms, but who also calls us to account and to sacrifice. Dietrich Bonhoeffer reminded his audience in 1937, as the poison of Nazism was about to spill all over the world, that "When Christ calls a man, he bids him come and die." Allen also warns us: "We do not proclaim the story of Superman. We tell the story of Jesus, the suffering servant, whose power is entirely different from the principalities and powers of a world of bondage." We must tell our children the story of the Lamb of God who takes away the sins of the world. This same Lamb calls us to take up our cross daily and follow him, all the way to Gethsemane, Golgotha, and beyond.

This is the God our children must come to know.

---

[1] Jaroslav Pelikan, *Jesus Through the Centuries: His Place in the History of Culture* (New York: Harper & Row, 1985) 1-8.

[2] Pelikan, 2.

[3] This book grew out of three separate nation-wide research projects on adolescent spirituality conducted between 1990 and 1993. Altogether, over 4,000 teens, drawn proportionally from throughout the United States in accordance with regional Church of Christ populations, participated in the projects. See also endnote 2 in Chapter Three.

[4] Pelikan, 3.

[5] Leonard Allen, Portraits of God: Abilene Christian University's Youth and Family Conference, Feb. 1991.

3

TEENS AT RISK: DIAGNOSING SPIRITUAL VULNERABILITY

Rebecca was an astounding bundle of joy. God answered her adoptive parents' prayers when he sent the five-day-old Rebecca home with them. After her parents had agonized for years at not being able to bear their own children naturally, they, their family, and their community of faith were thrilled with the baby's arrival.

As Rebecca grew older, the family also grew together. Yet because her adoption had been legally "closed" and because they felt they had little in common with the girl's biological parents, her adoptive parents shared very little with her about her adoption or her biological family history. Rebecca's parents were sure that their love and their family's commitment to God would provide Rebecca all the security she would need. And Rebecca did seem to grow up happy and contented within her Christian home.

At age 16, however, she changed radically. Her parents discovered to their dismay that she was sneaking out of the house late at night, regularly drinking alcohol, and having sex with her boyfriend. When they confronted her, Rebecca was defensive and defiant. Desperate for help and unable to explain Rebecca's changes, her parents sent her to a counselor. Yet her behavior didn't improve. Upset about being sent to therapy, she simply rebelled more throughout high school, seeming to abhor all that was sacred to her parents. Her bitterness turned to depression and, finally, after Rebecca burned her arms with cigarettes and attempted to kill herself, her parents placed her in a hospital for emotionally disturbed teens.

The real seeds of Rebecca's anger, confusion, and rage were discovered through this hospital care. Rebecca had for years suppressed feelings of being abandoned and rejected by her biological parents, and it was not until she was in high school that these feelings erupted. Despite her loving parents and a wonderful church community, Rebecca's chronic sense of inferiority and rejection traumatized her.

We do not tell the story of Rebecca to cast doubt on the beauty and blessing of adoption. Rather, her experience highlights one of several possible factors in the lives of our children which serve as signals of potential danger. Rebecca's problem wasn't so much her adoption as her low self-esteem and her troubled relationship with Mom and Dad. Feeling bad about oneself is just one of a number of conditions which are predictive of adolescent spiritual crisis. Difficult parental relationships, a pile-up of stressors, listening to negative music, sexual activity, alcohol or drug use, or friends that use these chemicals—any of these are potential signs of spiritual vulnerability, our research shows. In this chapter we survey some of the most important danger signals which every parent, youth worker, or church leader ought to know.

Compounded Stress

Stress can cause teens not to take God seriously. As we discuss further in Chapter Four, teens today feel immense pressure to grow up fast. Increasingly, it seems, they don't have opportunities to be *just* teens. Dr. David Elkind, Professor of Child Study at Tufts University, describes this state of affairs in his book *All Grown Up and No Place To Go: Teenagers in Crisis*:

> There is no place for teenagers in American society today—not in our homes, not in our schools, and not in society at large. This was not always the case: barely a decade ago, teenagers had a clearly defined position in the social structure. They were the "next generation," the "future leaders" of America. Their intellectual, social, and moral development was considered important, and therefore it was protected and nurtured. The teenager's occasional foibles and excesses were excused as an expression of youthful spirit, a necessary Mardi Gras before assuming adult responsibility and decorum. . . . In today's rapidly changing society, teenagers have lost their once privileged position. Instead, they have had adulthood thrust upon them. Teenagers now are expected to confront life and its challenges with the maturity once expected only of the middle-aged, without any time for preparation.[1]

As may be seen in Table 3.1, the teens in our survey confirm that their lives are not without worry or turmoil.

As we have researched adolescents over the last two decades we have learned that what wears teens down most often is not the particular stress they experience but rather the *accumulated, unreleased* stress. It seems teens can handle many stressful situations with resilience if they can consistently express their emotions or enjoy a rest between the stresses. But when, for whatever reason, the stresses pile up with no relief, teens may become depressed, think poorly of themselves, or act rudely.

SENIOR HIGH STUDENTS AND PILE-UP OF STRESSORS

1	Broke up with a close girlfriend/boyfriend	52%
2	Had trouble with teacher or principal	48%
3	Had major hassles with brother or sister	39%
4	Self or family member experienced conflict with someone at church	38%
5	Parent or sibling became very ill	36%
6	Have had suicidal thoughts	35%
7	Experienced significant conflict with parents	34%
8	Failed in one or more subjects at school	33%
9	Experienced significant depression	31%
10	Close friend died	31%
11	Have been drunk at least once in life	29%
12	Family member had trouble with alcohol	27%
13	Had significant illness or hospitalization for physical problem	25%
14	Parent lost a job	25%
15	Harassed sexually by anyone (people making sexual comments, etc.)	24%
16	Parent divorced or separated	22%
17	Frequently moved during childhood/adolescence	21%
18	Had family member with a mental illness	17%
19	Have become sexually active	15%
20	Experimented with illegal drugs	15%
21	Arrested for any reason	11%
22	Ran away from home	10%
23	Struggled with an eating disorder (anorexia, bulimia, etc.)	10%
24	Experimented with New Age or occult activities	7%
25	Sexually abused as a child	5%
26	Struggled over the fact of adoption	5%
27	Parent died	4%
28	Struggled with sexual identity (wondered about homosexuality)	3%
29	Had an abortion	2%
30	Brother or sister died	2%

TABLE 3.1

As we embarked upon this project we wondered if the pile-up of stress also affected adolescent spirituality. Our survey shows clearly that it does. Whether involving a normal bodily change or an unexpected loss of a parent, we found that the accumulation of stressful events predicts teens' taking God seriously *with more accuracy* than church attendance, family income, parental discipline, family communication, or even parents' ability to verbalize their love and appreciation for Christ.

Toxic Music

A second element that correlates to teens struggling spiritually is "toxic" music—types of music often referred to as heavy metal, rap, and grunge. When we speak of toxic music we mean modern music in which the lyrics repeatedly refer to murder, suicide, rape, illicit sex, or the pointlessness of life. In our earlier book, *Dying to Tell*, we reported that teens who frequently listen to classical, jazz, Christian, and pop music are more than twice as likely to be alcohol-free than teens who listen to heavy metal music.

We're certainly not saying that all popular music is destructive. To do so we would have to discredit some of God's most faithful workers who have composed and written beautiful works glorifying God. As Table 3.2 demonstrates, our research shows that there is a correlation between certain music groups and *higher* rates of adolescent spirituality.

HELPFULNESS OF GOD AND MUSIC

1	Christian music	84%
2	Classical music	79%
3	Oldies	73%
4	Soft rock	71%
5	Pop	68%
6	Country	67%
7	Cultural contemporary	65%
8	New Age	61%
9	Metal	59%
10	Speed metal	54%
11	Heavy metal	51%
12	Punk	39%
13	Black metal	30%

TABLE 3.2

We identified teens who say God is helpful to their lives, and then we sorted them according to the kind of music to which they listen. Of those teens who listen to Christian music, 84% find God helpful, compared to only 30% of those who listen to black metal. Note particularly what happens to the views of God among the teens who listen to speed metal, heavy metal, punk, and black metal (categories 10, 11, 12, and 13). Table 3.3, which offers a further breakdown of metal music, also necessitates a warning. The world of popular music is an ever-changing scene and the influence of one band may last only a few months—even, at times, only a few weeks. Talking to your teen about the bands listed in Table 3.3 may yield no response. At the moment, so-called "grunge" bands, such as Pearl Jam, Nine Inch Nails, and Soundgarden, are influential. Six months from now, they may not be. The important thing to realize is that although particular bands may wax or wane, themes of death, sadism, cruelty, and nihilism continue, regardless of the group currently espousing them. These destructive ideas are the real cause for concern.

"TOXIC" MUSIC IMPACTING ADOLESCENT SPIRITUALITY

Black metal music. Having either Satanic lyrics or Satanic symbols on the cover. Current examples of "black" metal music or satanic music are:

1	Slayer	**9**	Atheist
2	Venom	**10**	Obituary
3	King Diamond	**11**	W.A.S.P.
4	Satan	**12**	Death
5	Ozzy Osbourne	**13**	Merciful Faith
6	Testament	**14**	AC/DC
7	Candlemass	**15**	Megadeth
8	Cannibal Corpse		

Pure speed or metal trash. Having a very violent and aggressive or sadistic theme and heavily related to drug use among adolescents. Examples of speed metal music are:

1	Suicidal Tendencies	**6**	C.O.C.
2	D.R.I.	**7**	Meliah Rage
3	G.B.H.	**8**	Anthrax
4	Defiance	**9**	Deicide
5	GWAR	**10**	Nuclear Assault

Heavy metal music. Having a less frenzied and vicious theme, often closely related to adolescent substance use and abuse, and almost always related to defiant and recalcitrant attitudes. Examples are:

1	Cinderella	**5**	M.O.D.
2	Metallica	**6**	Stormtroopers of Death
3	Motley Crue	**7**	Pantera
4	Sepultura		

Metal music. Least dangerous of the aggressive music, yet remains also related to alcohol and drug use, as well as tendency to reject the call to spirituality. Examples of these groups are:

1	Def Leppard	**6**	Bon Jovi
2	Van Halen	**7**	Precious Metal
3	Poison	**8**	Vixen
4	Guns and Roses	**9**	Prince
5	L.A. Gun	**10**	Kiss

TABLE 3.3

Low Self-Esteem

Another category of spiritually-vulnerable teens is composed of those who feel badly about themselves. As we have often said, adolescence is by definition a time of intense emotional highs and lows. As their relationships, their responsibilities, and their bodies change, teens are in constant search of their identities. Most adults can recall times when it was possible to feel elation and depression almost simultaneously. These feelings are normal, but to teens they feel strange, painful, and isolating.

Some adolescents, however, struggle more than others. Some consistently feel bad about themselves. They picture themselves as weak or awkward, and they don't like what they see. Whether attributable to an obvious cause or not, these teens have rotten self-images. We had this group in mind when we wondered whether feelings of low self-esteem, depression, and alienation affect spiritual growth. Our study firmly reveals that teens who feel useless, unimportant, incompetent, or dissatisfied are much less likely to be serious about a personal relationship with God.

Figure 3.1 illustrates these findings. Perhaps it would be helpful at this point to explain the figures *throughout* this book. Several of the figures compare two factors: "X" and "Y." In Figure 3.1, for example, "importance of God" and "self-esteem" are compared. The chart shows *association, not necessarily causation.* Hence, reading the chart accurately, one could say, "Of the teens who rarely feel useful, only 35% believe God is truly important," or "Of the teens who believe they do many things well, 40% believe God is truly important." We are not empirically asserting which factor comes first or whether one *causes* the other. Our goal is to show an *association* between two factors or qualities. At times, however, we do use causal language because when certain associations appear consistently throughout several independent studies it is statistically legitimate and plausible (although not scientifically inevitable) to conclude that one factor gives rise to another. Thus, our present assertion is that if we help teens develop self-esteem, they are more likely to believe that God is important.[2]

IMPORTANCE OF GOD AND SELF-ESTEEM

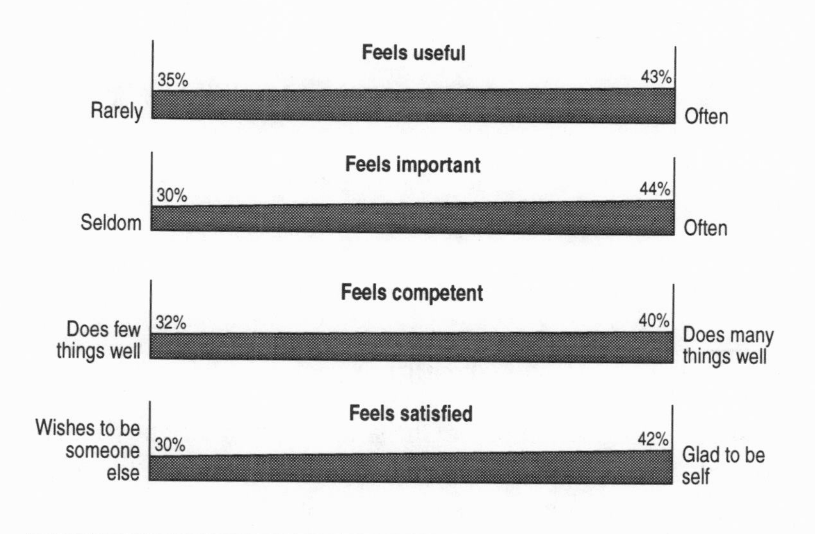

FIGURE 3.1

We also find a direct relationship between teens' view of themselves and their view of God. The more teens are satisfied with themselves, the more they value God, and vice versa. For example, 75% of those teens who value themselves also value God and his helpfulness, compared with only 49% of those who do not value themselves (Figure 3.2).

This pattern continued when we compared teens' agreement with specific statements and their appreciation of God. Teens who say things such as, "I am easy for people to get close to," "I can be counted on and trusted," and "I am a competent person," are much more likely to value God. Conversely, teens who feel insecure in these areas take God less seriously.

HELPFULNESS OF GOD AND PERSONAL SATISFACTION

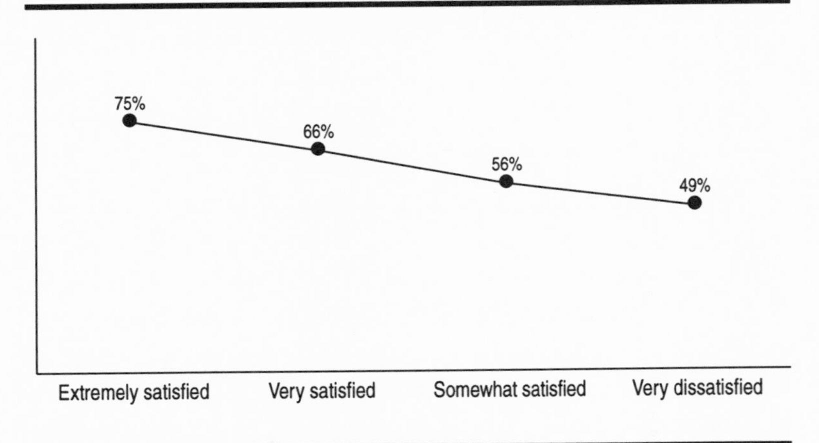

FIGURE 3.2

We understand that Christianity's primary business is not self-help or promoting the power of positive thinking. Promoting self-esteem is not our primary concern as Christian parents, either. However, we are confident that a true Gospel is a healthy Gospel. It restores souls *and* psyches. In fact, the Greek word for "soul" is—*psyche*. When Christians experience God's presence and his gracious forgiveness, they are likely to feel better about themselves.

What should be the central mission of parenting and ministry to youth? To increase positive self-regard—to create a climate in which God can be accepted and loved—or to encourage our teens to know and obey the God of Scripture, hoping the child will achieve a proper self-regard in the process? We suspect this is another case of the chicken and the egg, and we suggest that we break out of the severe limitation of this either/or framework. We maintain that teaching children self-worth and teaching them to know God are not mutually exclusive strategies.

Men and women in the Bible who know God often reveal a breathtaking boldness and confidence. In sharing the good news we simultaneously declare God's greatness and the value of his human creatures. The price of an object determines its worth, observes Bruce Narramore. If a human being is purchased by the blood of the Savior, then surely human worth is settled and sure.

We should, however, be clear about the origin and source of our worth. *Self*-regard is hollow and elusive if it is not founded on *God's* regard for his creatures. A child who knows she is forgiven, beloved, and chosen should feel good about herself. Any child who doesn't have this sense of dignity, we argue, is in spiritual danger. Our final goal is not to use techniques to build the sad child's self-esteem. Our final goal is to help her know God in a proper way. Yet, development of the child's self-regard may be a preliminary and instrumental goal. A child who rejects herself, who feels abandonment and self-contempt, may dwell in such a deep well of despair that she cannot profitably hear the Word of God. Perhaps she must hear the "good news" that she is worth the bother before she can hear the Good News that Jesus is her redeemer. If someone today is so despondent that she does not know her celestial pedigree, she may need to learn that great truth first. After all, all preaching in the Bible *presupposes that lost humanity is worth the bother.*[3]

For centuries, Christians have acknowledged the notion of "prevenient grace"—the grace that comes first, before we ever make a countermove toward God. Some of us have experienced this "grace before grace" in a loving parent, a faithful spouse, or some "chance" encounter that mysteriously led to a formal hearing of the Gospel. Healthy self-regard is one possible form of prevenient grace. Perhaps the initial preparation of the child's heart—one that despairs of its own significance—must come through someone (a parent, minister, or friend) conveying the gentle message, "You are loved. You are God's offspring. You are worth infinitely more than you can imagine." This is not the end of the Gospel, but it may be the beginning.[4]

Sexual Activity

As we noted in Chapter Two, about 66% of the teens we surveyed report that Jesus does make a difference in their sexual behavior. Yet those teens who are not sexually chaste form another group which is particularly vulnerable to spiritual crisis, especially regarding their relationship with Christ. Our research clearly shows that sexually active teens turn to Christ much less than those who are virgins. For example, as shown in Figure 3.3, 56% of virgins consult Christ in regard to cheating in school, while only 26% of sexually promiscuous teens do the same.

Additionally, it is not only those teens who willingly admit to their sexual activity who may struggle with Christ's lordship. While "churched teens" consistently report an unusually high rate of virginity (72%), many practice "technical chastity"—they participate in sexual gratification such as oral sex or mutual masturbation, but they stop short of actual penetration. These teens often have low self-esteem just like their peers engaged in intercourse. In turn, their relationship with Christ suffers. Remarkably, those who are truly virgins and who abstain even from "mutual touching" are *up to twice as likely* to allow Christ to influence them than are their "technically chaste" counterparts, as Figure 3.4 illustrates.

SEXUALITY AND LORDSHIP

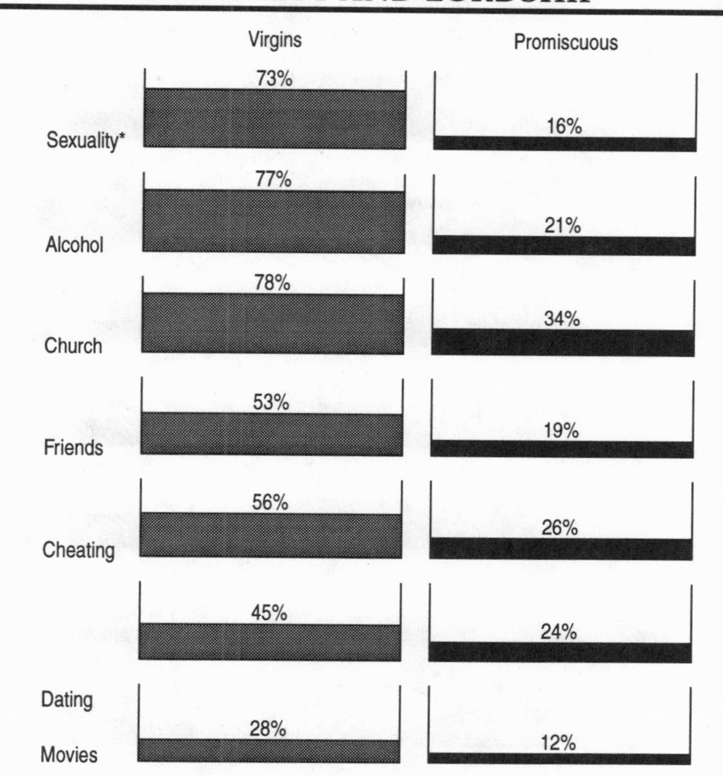

* Christ makes a difference on sexuality issues for 73% of virgins, but for only 16% of teens who would consider sex again regardless of commitment or relationship.

FIGURE 3.3

TECHNICAL CHASTITY AND LORDSHIP

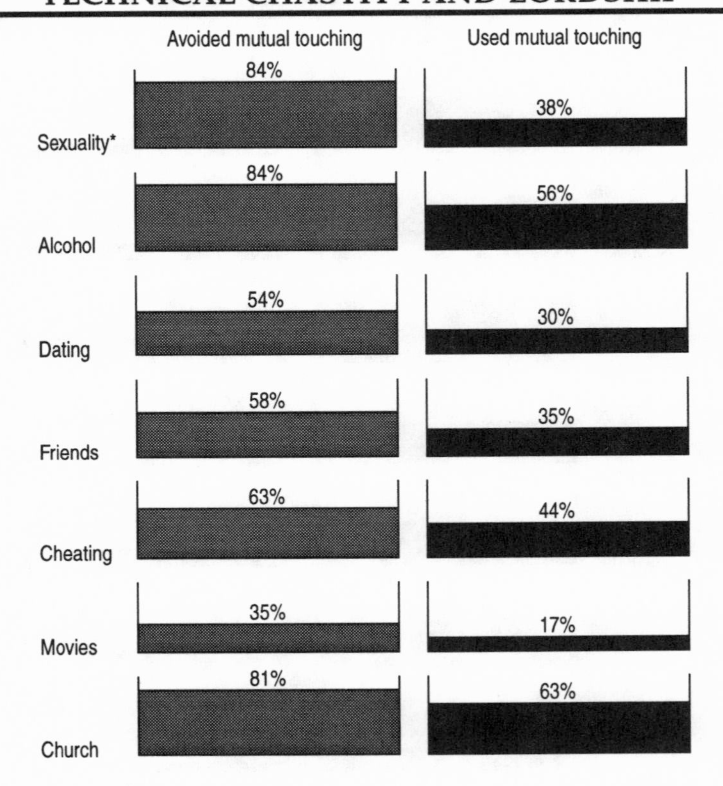

* Christ makes a difference on sexuality issues for 84% of teens who have never used mutual touching as a substitute for intercourse, but for only 38% of teens who frequently use mutual touching.

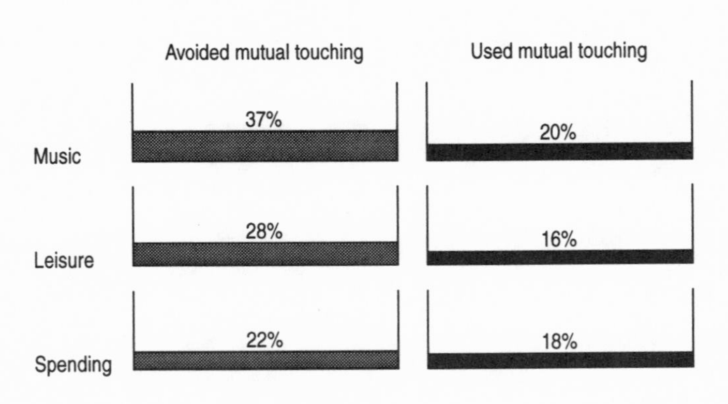

FIGURE 3.4

Substance Abuse

Not surprisingly, as Figure 3.5 shows, teens who use drugs are also at high risk of suffering spiritually due to a poor relationship with Christ. Our research affirms that these same patterns also occur with teens who use alcohol or drugs.

DRUGS AND LORDSHIP

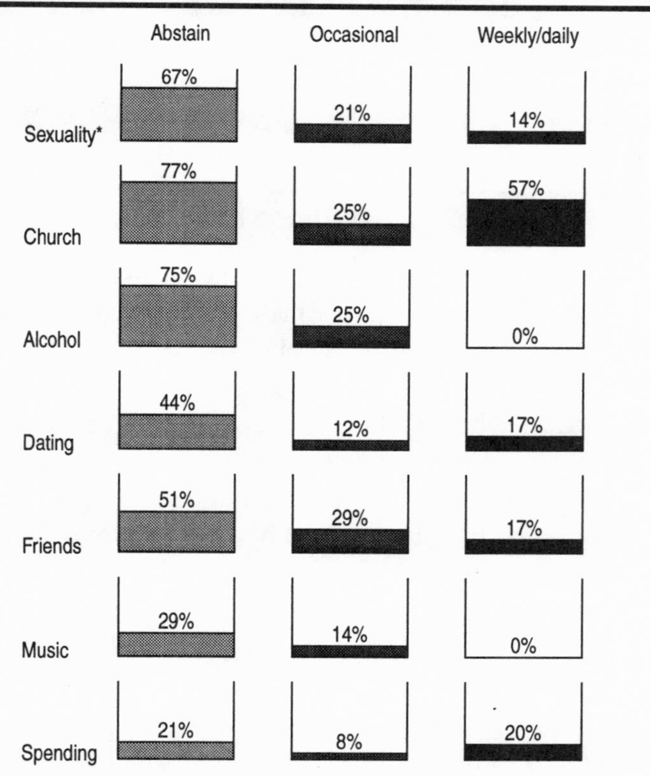

* Christ makes a difference on sexuality issues for 67% of teens who never use drugs, but for only 14% of teens who use drugs weekly or daily.

FIGURE 3.5

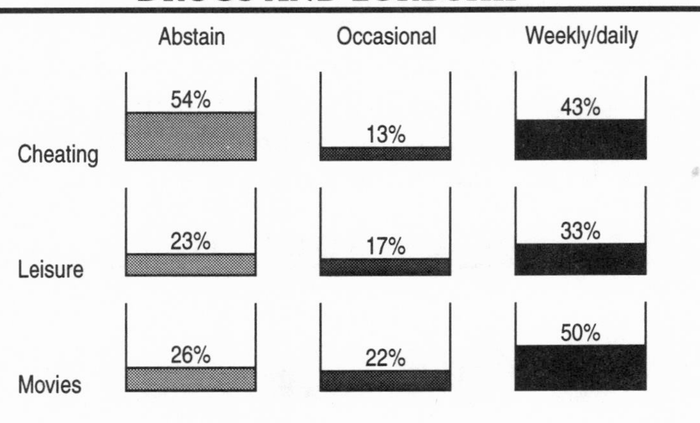

FIGURE 3.5

It is particularly alarming that teens who use drugs weekly or daily report that Christ does not *at all* influence their decisions concerning alcohol or their choice of music. Additionally, less than 20% report that Christ makes a difference in whether they are sexually active, whom they date, and whom they choose as friends. As with premarital sex, those teens who abstain from chemical substances are much more likely to be affected by Christ than those who do not.

Alcohol among Friends

There is also another dimension to the spiritual vulnerability of teens who abuse alcohol and drugs. We have found during past research that when a teen's close friends drink regularly, that teen is also very likely to do the same. Our study shows that among teens whose close friends drink, *80% drink themselves.* Likewise, of the teens whose best friends abstain, *only 10% drink regularly.*

Additionally, as Figure 3.6 shows, of the teens whose best friends refuse to drink at all (in other words, none of their friends drink), 45% state that God is the most important issue in their lives, whereas only 21% make that statement if most of their friends use alcohol.

IMPORTANCE OF GOD WHEN FRIENDS USE ALCOHOL

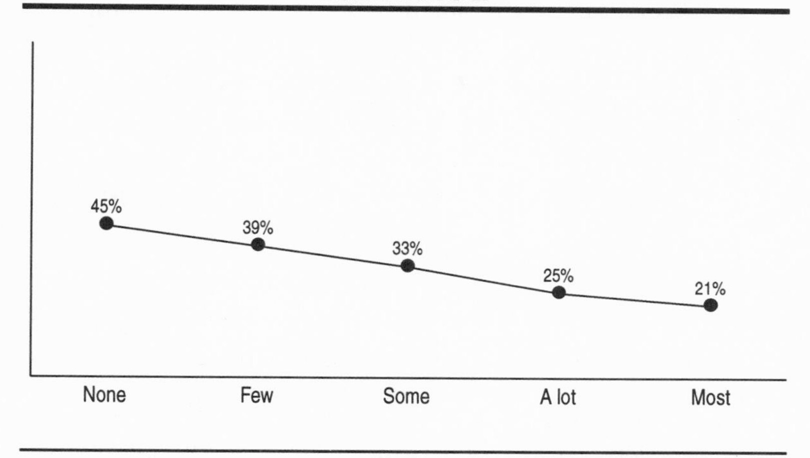

FIGURE 3.6

The same pattern occurs with drug use. Teens' choices of friends are closely related to faith issues. This fact is important to remember when considering which teens are spiritually vulnerable.

Adoption

We began this chapter with the story of Rebecca. While Rebecca's primary problem was not her adoption, but rather her troubled relationship with her parents and her profound feelings of abandonment, we return to her case because she represents an unusually vulnerable group of adolescents. Although only six percent of our sample were adopted, we found that they represent an important group of teens who face special problems. We must be candid. Compared to teens who are not adopted, the adopted teens appear much more at risk. This is not a reason to discourage adoptions. Rather, it is a call to be sensitive to the special needs of these children. We have discovered four areas of danger:

1. *Sexual acting-out.* 48% of the adopted teens report having sexual intercourse at least once, compared to only 16% of the non-adopted teens. This means that within the Christian community *adopted teens are three times more likely to have had extramarital sex* than teens who were not adopted. Additionally, 78% of the adopted teens practice "technical chastity," compared to 52% of the non-adopted teens.

2. *Alcohol use.* While 55% of the non-adopted teens use alcohol, 68% of the adopted teens do so.

3. *Traumatic childhood memories.* 14% of adopted teens report they had significant childhood traumas (such as incest or other sexual abuse), while only four percent of the non-adopted teens report such memories.

4. *Difficult parental relationships.* Adopted teens are over 20% more likely than non-adopted teens to have strained relationships with their parents which result in increased conflict, a lack of trust, and poor communication.

Teens who act out sexually, use alcohol, recall childhood trauma, and have significant trouble with their parents are less likely to value God than teens who don't have these difficulties. It's not surprising, then, that only 21% of the adopted teens in our survey report that God is the most important issue in their lives, while 35% of the non-adopted kids describe God as most important. This 14% variance highlights the need to explore, understand, and effectively minister to the special needs of adopted teens.

Age and Gender

Before we conclude this chapter, we would like to offer two informational asides. As we have analyzed youth culture for more than a combined half-century, we have wondered whether teens' spiritual formation varies depending upon age and gender. During the last four years, we have discovered some answers, particularly about teens' submission to Christ.

First, contrary to the popular assumption that as Christians grow older their dependence on Christ increases, we found that as most adolescents age they submit to Jesus less. For example, as Figure 3.7 exhibits, Christ makes a difference in the sexual decisions of 73% of those 12 years old or younger, compared with only 57% of those age 18 or older. Likewise, 84% of the 12-year-olds we surveyed consult Christ about drinking alcohol, while only 64% of the 18-year-olds do the same. It seems, sadly, that as teens approach the mid- to late teen years, they depend less on Christ.[5]

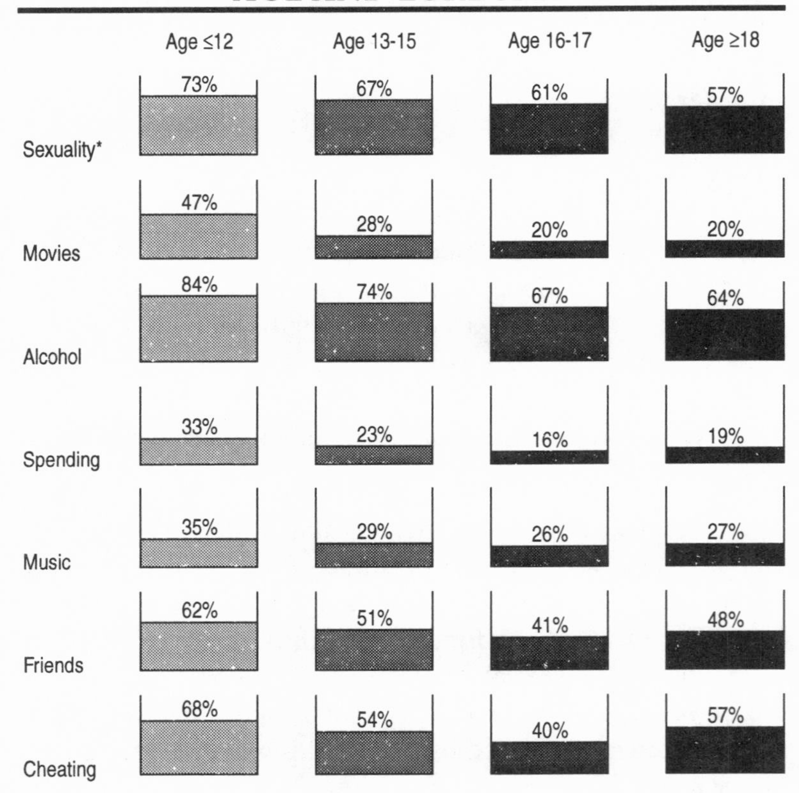

FIGURE 3.7

Second, it is also interesting to consider the differences between male and female adolescents in regard to their submission to Christ. We found that girls are anywhere from 2% to13% more likely to submit to Christ's lordship. Of the teens we surveyed, more girls than boys say Christ makes a difference in their decisions about dating, sexual activity, using alcohol, attending church, choosing music, and how to spend their time.

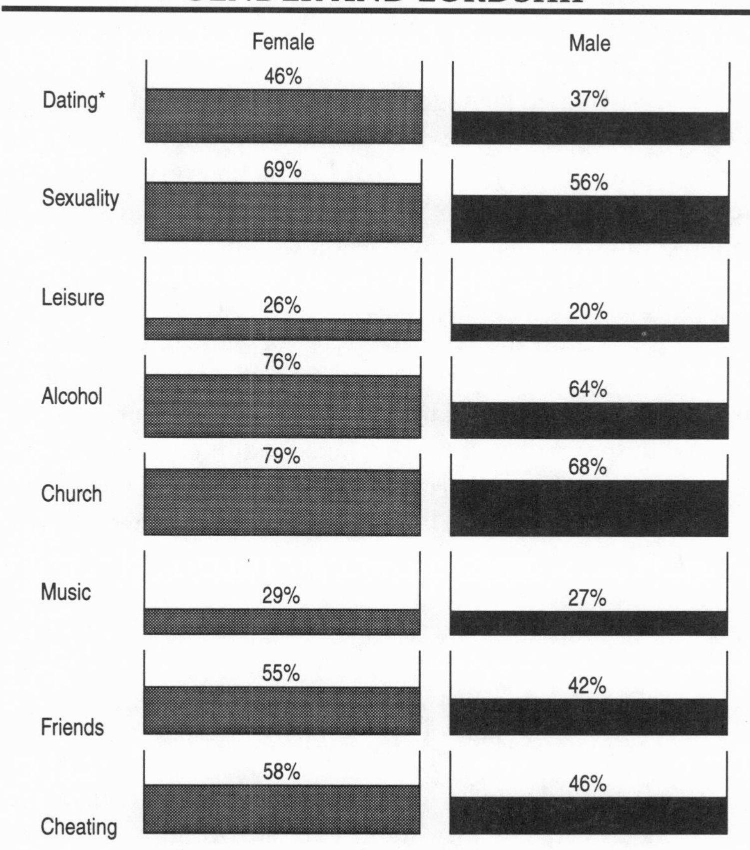

FIGURE 3.8

Conclusion

As we strive to parent and teach adolescents effectively, it is invaluable to remember what things have the greatest effect on teens. A pile-up of stressors, music steeped in negative themes, feelings of low self-esteem, alcohol use among friends, traumatic childhood memories, difficult parental relationships, and even the fact of adoption, do not necessarily *cause* spiritual crisis. That is not our argument. However, these elements are so often present in the lives of spiritually-troubled teenagers that we must be alert when any of them is present. We have good reason to suppose some of them contribute to spiritual malaise; at the very least their presence is symptomatic. Every wise parent and spiritual leader should at least recognize these factors as signals of potential spiritual danger.

We should model a lifestyle for our children that is not influenced by negative elements such as toxic music or the abuse of alcohol. We should be especially sensitive to the spiritual vulnerability of those who are adopted. In all cases, we need to act wisely by trying to minimize the factors which can detract from spiritual formation and emphasize those which enhance it.

---

[1] David Elkind, *All Grown Up & No Place To Go: Teenagers in Crisis* (New York: Addison-Wesley, 1984) 3.

[2] It should also be noted that all of the data presented in this book is statistically significant according to the laws of mathematical probability, and that it may be generalized based upon the stratified sampling of Church of Christ teens, a two-percent margin of error, and a confidence level of 99.9%. See also endnote 3 in Chapter Two.

[3] See Paul's presupposition in Acts 17 that the Athenians, even *before* conversion, are in fact sons and daughters of God.

[4] See Acts 17:24-29.

[5] See also our discussion of baptism and age in Chapter Seven.

4
Helping Teens Take God Seriously

Children have never been very good at listening to their elders, but they have never failed to imitate them. —James Baldwin

The family is the only institution in the world where the Kingdom of God can begin. —Elton Trueblood

Let parents bequeath to their children not riches, but the spirit of reverence. —Plato

The process of spiritual formation, the raising of children to know and love God, has long intrigued theologians and Christian educators. It is not always easy to know all the factors which help kids develop their own faith. Christian parents often dream of their children growing to know and love God. Yet as parents and youth workers we cannot merely *dream*. We must ask probing questions: How do children learn to know God? What kind of environment is actually needed to help kids grow spiritually? Who are the people to whom they listen when it comes to hearing the faith story? How do we most effectively assist teens in establishing their own vibrant faith?

The perplexing process of spiritual formation in the lives of our teens must go well beyond learning basic biblical stories and concepts, though this is important. In order to impact our adolescents spiritually, faith formation must address their deepest concerns, the roots of both their joy and their pain. When spiritual formation occurs, teens' perspectives, behaviors, values, and their very identities undergo radical change. The Scriptures speak directly about this reshaping of spiritual identity. The Apostle Paul indicates that "according to [God's] good purpose," spiritual formation requires the combined efforts of God, the individual believer, and a community of faith. Paul encourages the Philippians to "continue to work out your salvation [human effort] . . . for it is God who works in you. . ." (Philippians 2:12-13, NIV).

What exactly is the process of spiritual nurturing? In an effort to answer this question, we asked the teens in our three national surveys on spirituality to describe the types of relationships which seemed to be most significant to their faith. We wanted to know who the adults were who seriously affected their spiritual journeys. In addition, we asked them to tell us about the events in their lives which resulted in the development of their faith. Finally, we surveyed their practice of the spiritual disciplines. We begin with a profile of who helped them take God seriously.

Who Promotes Teen Spirituality?

We first asked a series of questions about the people who were influential in shaping the teens' beliefs in God. Table 4.1 displays their responses, in order of priority.

GREATEST INFLUENCES ON TAKING GOD SERIOUSLY

Adolescents within Churches of Christ were asked who most influenced their belief in God. The question was phrased, "Tell us who has most caused you to let God be important in your life." The following were mentioned in priority order:

1. Parents were the most important influencers of teen spirituality. 69% of all respondents mentioned one or both of their parents as the primary influencers of their faith.
2. Youth ministers were the second most often mentioned influencers of teen spirituality, with 11% listing their youth minister as the most significant person in their spiritual development.
3. Church friends were the third most often mentioned influencers of teen spirituality, with 7% stating that church friends were the most powerful influencer of their propensity to take God seriously.
4. Grandparents were the fourth important influencers of teen spirituality, with 5% of the teens mentioning their grandparents as the primary influencers.
5. Siblings were the fifth most important influencers of teen spirituality, with 4% stating that either a brother or sister was the primary force in helping them to take God seriously.
6. Aunts and uncles were the sixth most important influencers of teen spirituality, with 3% stating that these members of their extended families were the most important person.
7. Adult mentors (volunteer young adult youth leaders in local churches) were the seventh most important influencers of teen spirituality, with 2% of the teens in this survey mentioning them.
8. Teachers at church were the eighth most important influencers of teen spirituality, with 2% stating that their teacher at church most significantly influenced them to take God seriously.
9. Preachers at church were the final sources mentioned as influencers of teen spirituality, with 1% stating that they were most influenced by their preacher.

While preachers, teachers, mentors, church friends and extended family appear to be potential influencers, it appears from these data that the primary influencers are parents and youth ministers, with 80% mentioning either parent or minister to youth. These data provide powerful support for the dual focus of youth and family ministry.

TABLE 4.1

The table contains good news for parents who often wonder about their ability to contribute their own teens' spirituality. *Almost 70% of our teens report their parents as the primary spiritual influence in their lives.* Parents would do well to remember that adolescence by definition is a profound time of separation and identity development. Teens may not express themselves as openly as they once did, yet teens are open to influence. Adolescence necessarily demands more energy and creativity on the parents' part to stay overtly connected with the teen. It is encouraging to know that when teens feel discouraged or in despair, they listen to and watch their parents, although few teens would freely admit it. Our surveys consistently indicate that parents dramatically shape the spiritual lives of their children, for good or evil. As David Gelman notes,

> Sociologists have begun to realize in fact that teens are shaped more by their parents than by their peers, that they adopt their parents' values and opinions to a greater degree than realized.[1]

In general, no one is more powerful or influential than parents!

In second place with 11%, youth ministers rank higher than church friends, other relatives, or other adult church leaders among those who help kids take God seriously. Periodically, church leaders wonder about the necessity and effectiveness of their youth ministry programs. Yet our own teens indicate that youth ministers perform an important role—they are second only to parents in spiritual influence.

It is essential that youth ministers understand just how influential they are in the lives of teens. In fact, they have a legitimate and necessary role in church ministry. Youth ministers must never see their positions as inferior to other ministers. The time has come to abandon any notion that youth ministry is a "step-child" to "more important" ministries. The truth is that youth ministers may be more important to the spiritual lives of adolescents than all of the other ministers combined, though of course all ministries can fit together to provide the best possible setting for spiritual formation. Further evidence of the influence of youth ministers comes from two additional national surveys reported in our earlier works *Shattering the Silence* and *Dying to Tell:*

- Among teens who find youth ministry extremely helpful, 80% are virgins, compared with a 58% virginity rate among those who devalue youth ministry.
- 73% of teens who value youth ministry abstain from alcohol and drugs, compared with a 42% abstinence rate among teens who devalue youth ministry.
- When youth activities were seen as "very helpful" among adolescents, their alcohol and drug abstinence rate was 80%, compared to only 29% among those who found youth activities "not helpful."
- Among the top 10 places teens would go for help with an alcohol or drug problem, youth ministers ranked third behind family members and friends, but significantly ahead of counselors, other ministers, and physicians.

Youth ministers should in no way supplant parents, but youth ministers' role of teaching and encouraging spiritual development among our youth is essential.

We find two necessary ingredients in churches that have youth programs which successfully foster commitment to God and to the community of faith. First, in these congregations youth ministry is elevated to an important place, avoiding the "step-child" syndrome. This involves realistic and adequate budgeting for youth ministry activities, parental commitment of time and energy, strong leadership, adequate strategic planning, and significant activities. Church leaders clearly articulate ministry goals, and leaders audit the curriculum to insure that class materials are relevant and biblical. Most important, leaders devote themselves to prayer for their young people. In summary, we can say a successful church is *committed* to its youth.

A second ingredient involves strengthening fundamental parenting skills. We must go beyond occasional sermons and classes in order to develop extensive programs that teach fathering, nurturing, discipline, marital strengthening, financial planning, family decision-making, conflict management, stress management, family activities fostering spirituality, and family devotionals. The best possible approach is one in which youth ministers or family ministers combine their experience, love, commitment, and knowledge to care for their young. Parenting and youth ministry are both vital to adolescents. Teens benefit most when these two missions support each other rather than compete with each other.

In its early days, youth ministry emphasized adolescent separation from their families, perhaps in an attempt to provide relevance and cohesion, or perhaps in response to the 1950's and -60's culture which stressed independence and exclusion as a gateway to personal meaning. We realize now how misguided this approach was, for our research overwhelmingly supports the recent trend to involve parents in the work of faith development. This broader focus, sometimes called "youth *and* family ministry," demands that the church minister both to adolescents and their parents. This united approach will be an essential element for effective adolescent ministry into the twenty-first century.

When we asked teens to list those most influential in their decisions to commit their lives to Christ through baptism, once again they cited the same individuals. More specifically, mothers were at the top of the list at 76%; fathers followed at 68%; and youth ministers were closely behind at 65%. Elders were mentioned by only one percent of our teenagers as having a significant influence on decisions for baptism. This low response for the church leaders has been a consistent finding in our research. Sadly, many of those who have been called to know and lead their sheep appear to have almost no influence.

Recently, Christians have debated the place of elders, teachers, and pulpit ministers in spiritual formation. It would be an inappropriate use of our research to devalue any form of church leadership. Teachers and preachers can facilitate faith formation and can play a dynamic part, although their function is not always obvious and direct. Of course, we have no way of estimating the value of the long-term faithfulness of Bible teachers and preachers which might influence a teen's decision to commit his or her life to Christ. All mature Christians have been the beneficiaries of invisible and forgotten guides. As the respected Abilene Christian University administrator and mentor, A. B. Morris, once observed, "We eat fruit from others' trees, and drink water from wells we didn't dig." He reminds us that faith development is a process, involving many kinds of people and church experiences.

Qualities of Spiritual Mentors

How is it that some adults seem so significant in the faith formation of teens while others appear to have little, if any, impact? Our research might discourage some adults since they may infer that their impact on the lives of adolescents is minimal. We must resist rash generalizations. Our surveys indicate that our effectiveness with teens is clearly connected to how we relate to them. Neither titles nor congregational roles are at issue, but rather personal qualities.[2]

Adolescents in our study were asked to describe the qualities of adults that they most respected and wanted to emulate. Table 4.2 lists the top twenty qualities that teens most admired.

QUALITIES OF EFFECTIVE MENTORS

Adolescents in the study were asked to describe the type of adult that they most respected and wanted to be like. The following were the top twenty characteristics or qualities that teens most admired.

1 Accepts me and is able to be supportive of me no matter what I do
2 Makes me feel special and valuable even when I don't believe it
3 Is able to be a friend without being too much of a buddy
4 Is patient even when at times I'm sure I drive him/her crazy
5 Is sensitive to my own hurts and never devalues my feelings
6 Is willing to listen before giving advice
7 Understands and makes you think he/she has been there before
8 Bright; seems to have thought through the tough questions about God and can answer my questions
9 Not afraid to touch me and tell me that he/she cares
10 Treats me with dignity
11 Makes me feel that my ideas are worth something
12 Is not embarassed to talk about his/her own relationship with God
13 Is noticeably confident without being arrogant
14 Is willing to share how God has been his/her strength
15 Is consistent; makes you feel he/she will always be there
16 Really seems to care about what I think; encourages me to make up my own mind
17 Talks to me at my level, but never talks down to or belittles me
18 Is willing to put me first; is generous and giving
19 Is honest and able to share his/her own struggles with me
20 Makes me think that there is no such thing as a stupid question

FIGURE 4.2

This is an important list for us to review. Parents and youth workers in previous years have gained insight by taking this chart and letting their own adolescents evaluate them on each item, using some kind of rating scale such as the one below:

5 = True of me *almost all* of the time,

4 = True of me *most* of the time,

3 = True of me *some* of the time,

2 = *Rarely* true of me,

1 = *Never* true of me.

Allowing adolescents to do such an evaluation can provide vital feedback about the effectiveness of parents and teachers. Some very good news arises at this point. It appears that *anyone* who has a heart and passion for the spiritual development of teens can connect in powerful ways with today's youth. Notice just how the qualities listed in the chart above are similar to Paul's summary of mature love:

> Love is patient, love is kind. It does not envy, it does not boast, it is not proud. It is not rude, it is not self-seeking, it is not easily angered, it keeps no record of wrongs. Love does not delight in evil but rejoices with the truth. It always protects, always trusts, always hopes, always perseveres. (1 Corinthians 13:4-7, NIV)

Our teens are actually telling us nothing unique when it comes to developing relationships. They are re-emphasizing a central biblical axiom. "And now these three remain: faith, hope and love. But the greatest of these is love" (1 Corinthians 13:13, NIV). Love never fails to understand.

Our surveys convince us some adults possess an unusual ability to interest kids in spiritual matters, while others are simply unable to do so. What explains this difference? During our three years of research, we interviewed hundreds of unchurched adolescents. We asked them to comment on the type of adult it would take to engage them in spiritual dialogue. Who will they listen to? Who will interest them in spiritual matters? Here is what they told us:

1. *Someone who takes God seriously.* Teens need adults who have spiritual integrity. Adults cannot share something with teens which they do not have or understand themselves. The adults who will actually help adolescents shape their own faith in God must themselves have a deep faith. Adults who just "pontificate" provide rebellious teens an excuse to exclude God. Our teens have a keen eye for hypocrisy. If our own stories of faith are not told with authenticity, adolescents will severely discount our testimony.

2. *Someone who is open, warm, and accepting of others.* Adolescence is a time of significant mental, emotional, and physical change. It is usually a period of "dizziness," when teens find trusting particularly difficult. They search for their own identities, apart from their parents'. This pulling away is typically accompanied by a wide range of troubling emotions, such as identity confusion, depression, extreme highs and lows, value questioning, irritability, and fears. Some of these ordeals are understandable to adults and others appear irrational. But to the teen these emotions are connected to major life issues. If we hope to aid and comfort our teens, we must give them our greatest empathy and tolerance.

3. *Someone who is non-judgmental.* Being non-judgmental does not indicate that one does not have firm and uncompromising values. Rather, it means that in any case of conflict between the ideal and sin, the adult's role does not include judging. We must be like Jesus with the woman caught in

the act of adultery. This woman was already judged in her own eyes, and that was enough for Jesus. His non-judgmental attitude shows us that our *beginning* point is not to preach, rebuke and censure, but rather to offer grace and understanding. Even when God's judgment against sin has to be pronounced, it is always to be done with tears. Like Jesus, we too must offer mercy while setting high standards, boundaries, and expectations.

4. *Someone who is willing to listen and ask guiding questions instead of lecturing.* It's often more effective with teens to ask, probe, and explore. Many times adolescents will better remember a lesson that came through personal struggle than a lesson merely spoon-fed to them. Indeed, it is Socrates whom we credit with this teaching style—asking questions so students might discover and teach themselves. Dumping a prefabricated answer or "parental truth" in the lap of an adolescent will often lead to rejection. Henri Nouwen advises:

> Our first task is not to offer information, advice, or even guidance, but to allow others to come into touch with their own struggles, pains, doubts, and insecurities—in short, to affirm their life as quest.[3]

Our research indicates that those adults who talk *with* a teen, rather than *to* a teen, are better received. Traditional lectures simply appear ineffective. Parents would do well to practice the spirit of Steven Curtis Chapman's lyrics:

Tomorrow morning when you wake up, and the sun does not appear,
I will be here. . .
I will be here when you feel like being quiet
When you need to speak your mind, I will listen
And I will be here when the laughter turns to crying
Through the winning, losing and trying, we'll be together,
'Cause I will be here.[4]

5. *Someone who is trustworthy.* Teens cherish a relationship with an adult in whom they can confide the most secret thoughts and fears of their hearts, knowing that all will be kept confidential. Kids are literally dying because of a shortage of trusting relationships. Adults must treat that trust as a sacred gift. Furthermore, teens need to feel that what was shared in the past has not been forgotten. We have personally witnessed adolescents receive great comfort when we gave them a hug and whispered a few words of encouragement such as, "I'm still praying for you. When can we talk again? We're going to keep working on this until God gives us a solution."

6. *Someone who practices forgiveness.* Forgiveness is fundamental to spiritual development. Frequently, all teens want after a crisis or failure is for somebody to say aloud words of absolution (i.e., "We all fail at some point," "I'm not mad at you," "I forgive you."). Moms, dads, youth ministers, elders, and Bible class teachers—are we

> not priests ourselves? Peter states that we are all part of a "royal priesthood" (1 Peter 2:9, NIV), called out of darkness into a marvelous light. Give our teens what they so desperately need: a word of forgiveness. Literally touch them, and *pronounce* forgiveness. Look them right in the eye and say, "You are forgiven. Go and sin no more." And if they say, "But it can't be that easy," explain that it is not easy at all. Remind them that their "sins have been forgiven on account of his name" (1 John 2:12, NIV). Tell them one more time the story of the cross. Tie the story of their pain to the story of redemption. It is when these two stories meet that the miracle of restoration occurs. This is the real meaning of truly "being Christ" to adolescents.

One of the unique features of Christ's ministry was his intuitive understanding of the human dilemma. John states that Jesus knew fully what it meant to "be a man." As Christ's ambassadors to adolescents, we are called to understand the adolescent dilemma. In this study we attempted to evaluate our ability as adults to appreciate such a dilemma. Specifically, we asked these teens to tell us what they believed most adults did not understand about their day-to-day struggles. Table 4.3 shows the responses.

THINGS ADULTS DO NOT UNDERSTAND ABOUT TEENS AND THEIR RELATIONSHIP WITH GOD

Adolescents in the study were asked to list those things that they believed most adults didn't understand about the day-to-day teen struggle to be faithful to Christ. The following were the top twelve issues that are most often not understood by adults within churches of Christ.

1. Teens need to be allowed and even encouraged to think independently. "Teens need the chance to decide for themselves what they believe and don't believe about God. You simply can't force a teen to take God seriously."
2. Teens need to be allowed to be teens. "Teens are not grown-ups' and they don't have the ability to take God as seriously as their parents do."
3. Teens think about God a lot. "Even when you would never dream, teens are thinking very seriously about God. Even when teens are not really into formalized religion, that doesn't mean they are not thinking seriously and frequently about God."
4. Teens typically don't trust adults with their doubts. "Most teens have a hard time feeling safe asking questions about God to adults."
5. Teens react negatively to spiritual pressure. "While parents and adults mean well, they have no idea what a turn-off it is to teens to be pressured into spiritual things.
6. Teens aren't impressed with a boring and impotent God. "Teens need a God who isn't all serious, and if there isn't some fun and excitement attached very few teens will be interested."
7. Teens need consistency. "Teens really need more than anything someone who is always there and who is willing to show us a life that is better than the one we know on the street."
8. Teens are not adults. "Parents' needs and teens' needs are very different at times, and teens refuse to be put into parents' 'God box.'"
9. Teens need limits and boundaries. "While teens are confused, searching and a bit rebellious, they really need and want some authority over them but don't know how to ask."
10. Teens are by nature volatile. "Adults don't understand or seem to tolerate much of teens' moodiness and the fact that God gave us our emotions in the first place."
11. Teens really want and deserve respect. "Teens have a lot more to contribute to the church than adults will ever allow."
12. Teens need nurturing most of all. "More than anything, teens need support and encouragement to live like Jesus lived."

TABLE 4.3

What can we learn from these issues? The list speaks for itself, but several parenting and teaching principles emerge from these concepts:

1. *Rightly or wrongly, teens feel themselves to be devalued.* Adults must go the second mile to show they respect teens. We do this best by devoting time to them, listening, and affirming them.

2. *Teens feel pressure to grow up fast.* Consider the media, peers, and some parents who push children into adult molds and expectations. This pressure creates confusion and builds resentment. Our children need activities and events that offer opportunities for creative expression. Kids need chances just to *be* kids and teens need opportunities just to *be* teens.

3. *Teens need adult attention.* The Lord says in Hosea: "When Israel was a child, I loved him. . . It was I who taught Ephraim to walk, taking him by the arms" (11:1,3, NIV). Our heavenly Father is attentive to his children. If we are to emulate him, we, too, must be attentive. Teens typically do not overtly affirm their parents and teachers, but they often feel more positively toward significant adults than they express. Adults who begin with a positive outlook toward adolescents, who spend time with them, and who value their comments and ideas, find themselves taken more seriously than adults who do not demonstrate these qualities.

   In our previous research, we have found significant correlations between "parent time" and adolescent "acting-out" with sex and substances: parents who spent at least 30 minutes a day with their teens had children who were more than twice as likely to avoid sexual promiscuity and regular use of alcohol than parents who spent little time with their teens. We cannot treat teens like small children, for there must be measured autonomy, but nurturing in appropriate ways is an essential ingredient in the "recipe" for a solid parent-child relationship.

4. *Teens need boundaries.* Teens will never declare to adults their need for limitations, but the need is clear. Frank discussions with adolescents about rules, accompanied by consistency and understanding, usually bring positive results. We may hope that one day our children will repeat these words: "When I was a boy in my Father's house, still tender, He taught me . . . and [his words were] life . . . and health" (Proverbs 4:3,22, NIV).[5]

Events That Spark Faith

As we've asserted, spiritual growth is partly a matter of adult mentoring. But it's also a matter of teens' experiences. It's enlightening to discover which events most significantly contribute to the faith of teens. We asked the teens to consider how each of thirty-one church-related events had contributed to their faith development. The teens responded to the following statement: "After thinking about your years in junior high and senior high, please evaluate each event as to its ability to positively influence you to take God seriously." It's important to note that Table 4.4 reflects the responses of older adolescents who have already graduated from high school. These older teens were far more able to evaluate these typical youth ministry events than those in early and middle adolescence.

MOST SIGNIFICANT EVENTS FOR FAITH DEVELOPMENT

The following events are listed in priority order as most contributing to teenagers' developing their own personal faith.

Scale:	5	4	3	2	1
	Extremely important	Very important	Somewhat important	Of little importance	Not important

	Event	Score
1	Summer mission trips	4.1
2	Summer camps	4.1
3	Youth retreats	4.0
4	Sunday morning Bible classes	3.9
5	Sharing God with mother	3.9
6	Individual Bible study	3.9
7	Youth devotional experiences	3.9
8	Special group prayer times	3.9
9	"Huddle" and "Life Group" experiences	3.8
10	Family camps	3.8
11	Sharing God with father	3.8
12	Significant crises	3.8
13	Sunday morning worship experiences	3.8
14	Ministry for rest homes or "senior saints"	3.8
15	Service projects	3.7
16	Sunday evening Bible studies	3.7
17	Kadesh, Encounter or similar camps at Christian colleges	3.7
18	Sunday evening worship services	3.7
19	Vacation Bible School	3.7
20	Father-teen events	3.7
21	Mother-teen events	3.6
22	Family devotionals	3.6
23	Special youth revivals or gospel meetings	3.6
24	Preaching	3.6
25	Mid-week Bible studies in homes	3.5
26	Special seminars	3.5
27	Winter ski trips	3.5
28	Family vacations	3.5
29	Wilderness Trek experiences	3.4
30	Special singing groups	3.2
31	Puppet ministry	2.8

TABLE 4.4

We are struck by the fact that mission trips and camps rank as the most important events in helping teens grow spiritually. This should be no surprise, since both events provide the adolescent with authentic community experiences. Mission trips, camps, and youth retreats all provide teenagers an extended setting in which genuine relationships can naturally develop. Consider this recollection of a youth trip to Colorado:

> The firelight flickers on thirty-five faces huddled around the campfire. As I study the faces around me—dirty and grimy from lack of bathing—I realize that an outside observer, not having experienced what we have just gone through, couldn't understand what we feel at this moment . . . All of us sit exhausted from our eight-hour hike, yet we don't complain. On the contrary, we feel joyous and fulfilled because today we finally made it to the very summit of the highest mountain in Colorado!
>
> I felt rather small and insignificant in comparison to the stark, almost harsh, yet beautiful wilderness of the mountain peaks. God's awesome creation stood silently, seeming indifferent to mankind . . .
>
> Finishing their unappetizing supper, my friends raise their voices in song. I look up at the stars and realize the necessity of close relationships—with one's self, with others, and with God. Through the support of my friends, and the strength of a personal relationship with God, I can overcome the challenges of life . . .
>
> The praising voices fill me with joy, and the smiles among the thirty-five faces reflect how close we have become. Soon, we will go back to the civilized world . . . But, I will return a different person.

Our research does not indicate that we should dismiss those events which did not rank as high. Remember that even the events at the bottom of the chart were at least somewhat important to the spiritual development of our teens. We do believe that a combination of people and events work together to nurture teens spiritually.

The Role of the Spiritual Disciplines and Faith

Finally, in our survey we discovered the great importance of spiritual disciplines to adolescent faith. We wondered, in fact, if spiritual disciplines would be considered or practiced by this computer-age generation. Table 4.5 lists the spiritual disciplines which teens report they practice.

SPIRITUAL DISCIPLINES MOST PRACTICED BY ADOLESCENTS

Teens Reporting Discipline	*Regular Practice of Discipline*
• Praise and celebration	38%
• Confession of sin/weakness	33%
• Serving others	23%
• Meditative prayer (honest, heartfelt searching for God)	21%
• Personal study	8%
• Weeping over the lost	6%
• Meditation on Scripture	3%
• Fasting	.9%

77% consider fasting unimportant
22% consider weeping over the lost unimportant
3-9% consider the other disciplines unimportant
50%-80% are ambivalent and lack discipline in practicing these spiritual disciplines

TABLE 4.5

We note that no single spiritual discipline is practiced by even 40% of our teens. Praise and celebration were the most practiced disciplines, followed by confession and service. Perhaps more alarming is the indication that fewer than 10% of our teens regularly engage in Bible study. The fact that less than six percent of our adolescents stated they "wept over the lost of the world," may indicate that this generation is not highly motivated to reach unbelievers. Additionally, almost a fourth of our teens considered "weeping over the lost of our world" completely unimportant! While meditation on Scripture is a biblical norm, as is fasting, both of these are almost non-existent in the daily lives of our teens. In addition to our teens' failure to practice the discipline of fasting, 77% of those surveyed stated that they believed such a practice is inappropriate!

In addition to the frequency of the spiritual disciplines, we examined the relationship between the frequency of teens' practice of spiritual disciplines and their belief that the Holy Spirit is essential in their lives. The data presented in Figure 4.1 shows how the spiritual disciplines affect teens' perceptions of the Holy Spirit working in their lives.

SPIRITUAL DISCIPLINES' IMPACT ON THE HOLY SPIRIT'S INFLUENCE ON TEENS

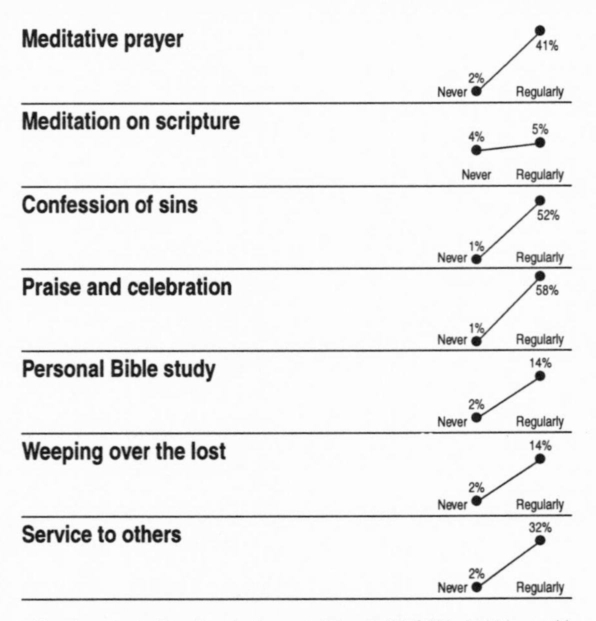

FIGURE 4.1

For those teens regularly practicing the discipline of meditative prayer, 41% stated that the Holy Spirit was absolutely essential to their spiritual walk. By contrast, among those who never practiced meditative prayer, only two percent stated that the Holy Spirit was absolutely essential to them. This correlation between spiritual disciplines and one's receptivity towards spiritual issues persists for all the remaining disciplines. Particularly great were the differences in the areas of confession of sins (52% compared with one percent) and praise and celebration (58% compared with one percent).

In our three years of research, the practice of spiritual disciplines was found to be *the most important of all the indicators of adolescent spirituality.* Evidently, there is no more important task for the youth and family minister than to provide instruction, example, and opportunities for kids to practice the spiritual disciplines. Herein lies a significant challenge. How does one sell a generation of MTV fans on the importance of regular prayer, Bible study and meditation?

The minister's task is do everything possible to minimize cultural barriers and impediments to faith and consistently model for our young people the joys of the disciplined life. Here are some practical suggestions that may help:

1. *Present the disciplines as normal.* Persist in presenting them as an expected part of the believer's life and not an "add-on" for the spiritually elite. Point out that Jesus spoke of prayer, fasting, and giving as if he fully expected his disciples to practice these disciplines.

2. *Encourage all the leaders of the church to model the disciplines.* Remember that our teens have verified over and over again that they are watching and listening. Disciplines are both taught and

caught. Imagine what an influence such consistent modeling would have over the lifetime of a teen in one's youth ministry. Deliberately practice spiritual disciplines from the time a teen enters the youth program as a middle schooler throughout his or her high school years. Encourage the disciplines in the earliest years of a child's life, being sensitive to what is appropriate at each age.

3. *Allow teens to personalize the disciplines.* While Jesus was persistent in his desire that all disciples devote their lives to prayer and fasting, nowhere did he provide an instructor's manual. Many young men and women have become disheartened because they were simply unable to emulate their youth minister's rising at 5:30 AM for quiet time, jogging for 10 miles while praying for the lost, and completing his Bible study before 7:00 AM. Follow Henri Nouwen's advice to "start small and keep it simple." A two-minute period of prayer and Bible reading that you keep daily is better than a one-hour devotional period that you end up abandoning.

We cannot prescribe a magic formula of spiritual formation. There is no simple checklist. Ours is not the duty of *doing* something *to* our teens, but rather of *being* something *for* them. Our teens need us badly—not our pat answers or our idealistic stories, but our genuine, authentic selves shaped in the image of Jesus. Yes, our teens need the body of Christ, working together to glorify him by nurturing our young "parts" into spiritual maturity, so that the body might shout even greater praise to the Lord on high.

While there is no plan which automatically yields spiritual maturity, there is a call. And it comes from our youth to us. They want their parents and their ministers involved in their lives. They want integrity, listening, and forgiveness. They want and need Christian fellowship and the spiritual disciplines. We can no longer avoid the cries of our adolescents. They are calling. And as surely as they call out in need, our God calls us to meet that need.

---

[1] David Gelman, "A Much Riskier Passage," *Our Times/2* Ed. Robert Atwan (Boston: St. Martin's Press, 1991) 49.

[2] See Chapter Eight for an extended discussion of mentoring.

[3] Henri Nouwen, *Seeds of Hope: A Henri Nouwen Reader* (New York: Bantam, 1989) 47.

[4] Steven Curtis Chapman, "I Will Be Here," *More to This Life,* Sparrow, 1989.

[5] See Chapter Five for further discussion of these principles.

5
Families That Help Teens

The only training which really matters is given within the home, and . . . there are no teachers so effective for good or evil as parents are. —William Barclay

The test of real fatherhood is not to try to be the ultimate father, but to point to the real One from whom reality comes. —Don Osgood

No discipline seems pleasant at the time, but painful. Later on, however, it produces a harvest of righteousness and peace for those who have been trained by it. —Hebrews 12:11

Over the last decade no other subject has received more emphasis than the American family. We appreciate the church's response to the failure of many families, but at the same time we are discouraged that the church has often sought to resolve this difficulty by secular, rather than theological, means. Churches are beginning to address family concerns, but we fear that family ministries are too often based on temporal psychological assumptions, rather than upon biblical truths. We believe family ministry must focus upon the relationship between God and the family.

We are concerned that modern social scientists seem to believe that if we could only eliminate the "dysfunctions," our families would be perfect. We know this is simply not true. We are sinners, and our families are, therefore, groups of sinners. "For all have sinned and fall short of the glory of God . . ." (Romans 3:23, NIV). We cannot eliminate all our shortcomings. We cannot reach perfection. In order to love our spouses fully and raise our children with true joy we must focus on him who redeems us, rather than on ourselves. Dr. Charles Siburt, Professor of Bible at Abilene Christian University, warns us to be on guard against naive, formulaic approaches to family therapy:

> Besides our theology of families being egocentric and self-indulgent (believing that God exists for us rather than we for him), it is often neurotic, perfectionistic, and at its center Pharisaical. You'll find that popular attempts to present a biblical theology of families consist of: "If you'll do this, it will all be better, there won't be as many heartaches, you'll be happier, and you'll have brighter and healthier kids." The idea is that God has it all worked out and if you are good disciples and just follow the plan you'll have a perfect family.[1]

God may not choose to eliminate all our earthly hurts. Yet only God can forgive us and bring us into relationship with himself and with a community of faith so that the pain in our lives may be consoled and eased.

We should be cautious when anyone offers us "secrets for effective and successful family living." Even in the Bible there is no "ideal" family. Families in the Bible are full of deceit and conspiracy and lust: Shem, Ham, and Japeth attempted to conceal their father's intoxication. Joseph's own brothers tried to assassinate him. Despite her pleading, Tamar was raped by her brother, Amnon. Lot's daughters slept with their father.

Modern psychologists would readily diagnose Adam and Eve, our first "models" of parenthood, as mentally unhealthy. For example, the *Diagnostic and Statistical Manual of Mental Disorders*, the guidebook psychologists use to diagnose dysfunctions, lists a problem in children called "Oppositional Disorder." The manual asserts that if four of the following seven traits are often observable in a child, the child is emotionally disturbed and should be placed in a mental hospital or in residential care:

If the child . . .

1. Has a problematic temper
2. Is argumentative with adults
3. Defies adult requests, doing things that annoy people
4. Blames others for his or her mistakes
5. Is touchy or easily annoyed by others
6. Is angry and resentful, spiteful or vindictive
7. Is unable to control language

Based on this list, Cain would surely be hospitalized in the 1990's.

We offer this hypothetical example simply to confirm that this chapter is not a "checklist" for forming the perfect family. Rather, it is a collection of information that can help us observe patterns within our families which may either help or hinder our teenagers' spiritual formation. Once we note these patterns, we can prayerfully alter them in a way that will lead our teens—indeed our entire families—closer to God.

The Role of Marital Satisfaction

Most of the teens we surveyed view their parents' marriage positively. Sixty-seven percent perceive their parents as "exceptionally happy" or "highly satisfied" in their marriages. Only five percent report parents who are "very unhappy" or "miserable" in their marriages.

Furthermore, 76% of our teens are members of "intact families" in which divorce or separation has never occurred or in which there is now a stable marriage. Only 24% live in divorced or separated homes, which compares favorably to the United States average of nearly 40%.

We wondered about the role marital satisfaction plays in adolescent spirituality. How do teens who consider their parents satisfied in marriage compare to those who believe their parents are dissatisfied? We found that church attendance is higher among the teens of maritally-satisfied parents than among those of dissatisfied parents. Attendance is also greater for intact families than divorced families. Additionally, 73% of the teens of satisfied parents believe God is important, while only 19% of the teens of unhappy or moderately happy parents believe the same.

Teens of maritally satisfied parents are also more likely to esteem God and consider what Jesus wants for their lives. In other words, there is a high correlation between good marriages and teens who consider God important and submit to Christ. Figure 5.1 shows that the teens of parents satisfied with their marriages are almost *15 times more likely* to take God seriously. In other words, of the kids whose parents are happily married, 73% of them report taking God seriously. By contrast, only five percent of the teens whose parents are unhappily married take God seriously.

IMPORTANCE OF GOD AND MARITAL SATISFACTION

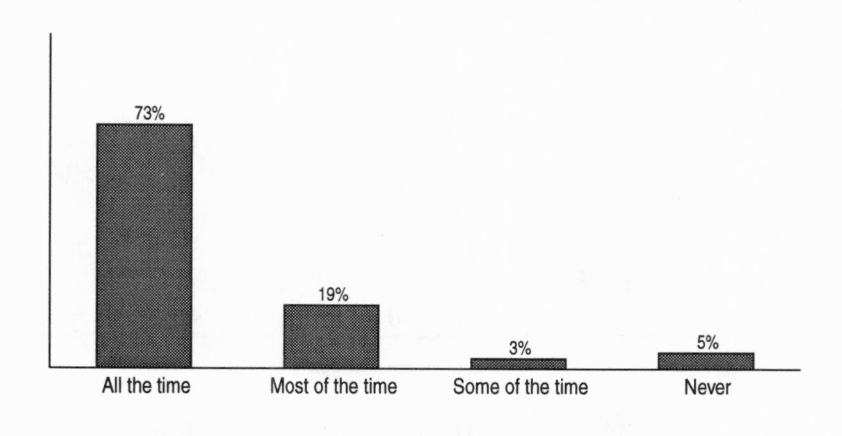

FIGURE 5.1

Sadly, some of us as church members and parents have focused so intensely on the "forest" of youth ministry that we have overlooked the "trees" of daily life which spiritually affect our teens. Although specific ministries centered on youth are important, positive family traits—such as consistent parenting skills, open communication, and parents' commitment to Christ—are most critical to the spiritual formation of teens.

We have witnessed this reality in our own community. Reg and Patty were happy members of a local church in which their two sons were active in the youth group. The whole family participated in the bus ministry. Yet Reg and Patty were upset that as their sons grew older, the boys began questioning their religious heritage. Reg and Patty lashed out at the church elders and youth minister, blaming them for what they perceived as a decrease in their sons' spirituality. However, the real source of their teens' spiritual quandaries, as the church later came to find out, was not the church's failure, but rather a chaotic home life fueled by neglect and verbal abuse in Reg and Patty's marriage. Sadly, the root of many adolescents' spiritual angst is this sort of marital failure.

Relationship with Parents

We also asked how much time the teens and their parents spent together and *how* this time is spent. The responses are insightful.

IMPORTANCE OF GOD AND FAMILY COMMUNICATION

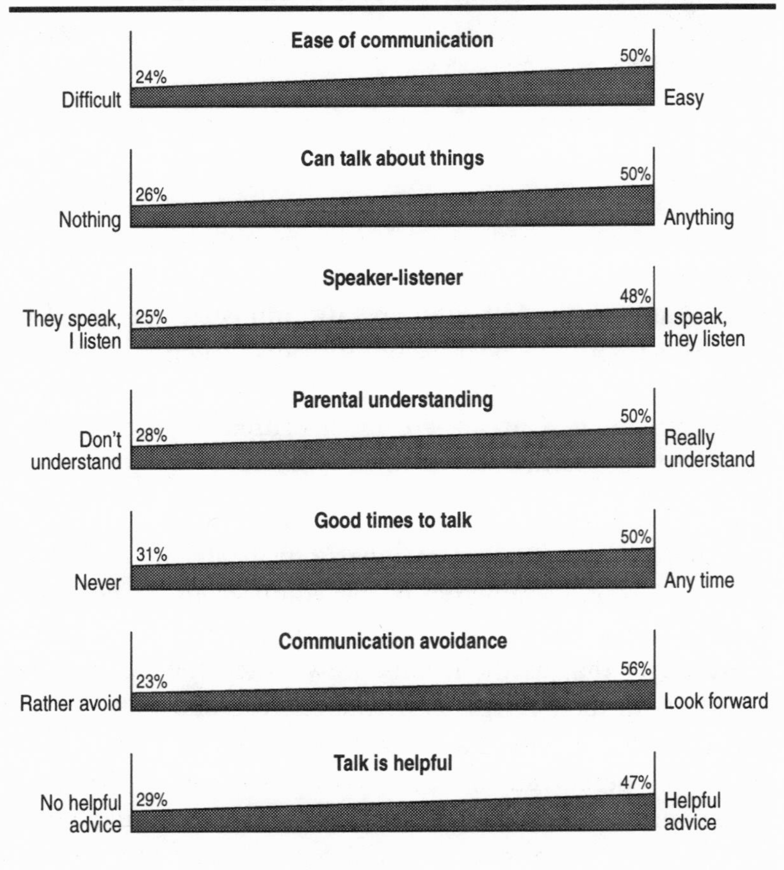

FIGURE 5.2

Parent-teen communication. Forty-four percent of the adolescents indicate "excellent" or "very good" communication within their families, while only 19% describe their family communication as "difficult" or "bad." In a number of family communication areas (i.e. "ease," "timing," "topics," "understanding," "helpfulness"), the majority of teens with positive family communication view God as important. For example, as Figure 5.2 indicates, teens who view communication within their family as "easy" are *twice as likely* to take God seriously as teens who view their family communication as "difficult." We parents need to remember that when we are talking with our adolescents, we are not involved in mundane matters. Our communication with our teens impacts their relationships with God.

Encouraging autonomy. Parents of adolescents are often frustrated when they realize they are not as powerful in the lives of their children as they were at one time. Family "government" changes during adolescence. While teens love the parents' declining power and control, parents often develop a mild case of paranoia. Watchful parents of younger children can prevent all sorts of abuse, injury, and trauma. But when parents pass the car keys, they also surrender much of their ability to protect their children. Yet we believe one of the primary responsibilities of parents is to teach their adolescents to be self-supporting and autonomous. Teens must learn to separate from their parents and to "test their own wings."

HELPFULNESS OF GOD AND ENCOURAGING AUTONOMY

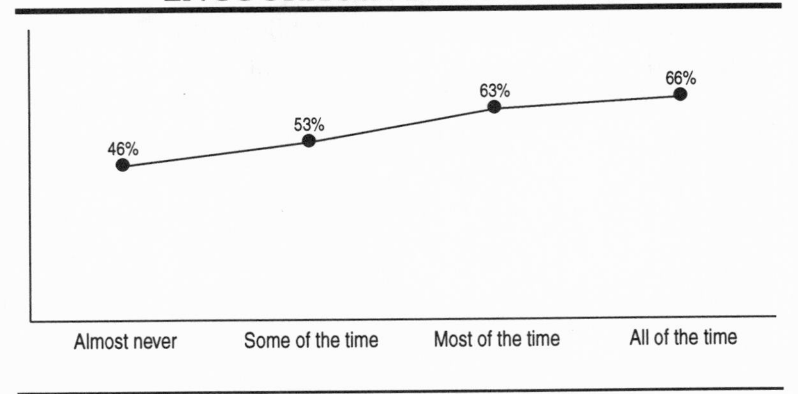

FIGURE 5.3

As Figure 5.3 confirms, teens who are granted reasonable personal autonomy are more likely to view God as helpful. For example, of the adolescents who say their parents "almost never" encourage the teen to be independent, only 46% say "God is helpful." However, of those kids who say their parents encourage autonomy "all of the time," 66% say "God is helpful."

IMPORTANCE OF GOD AND PARENTAL SUPPORT

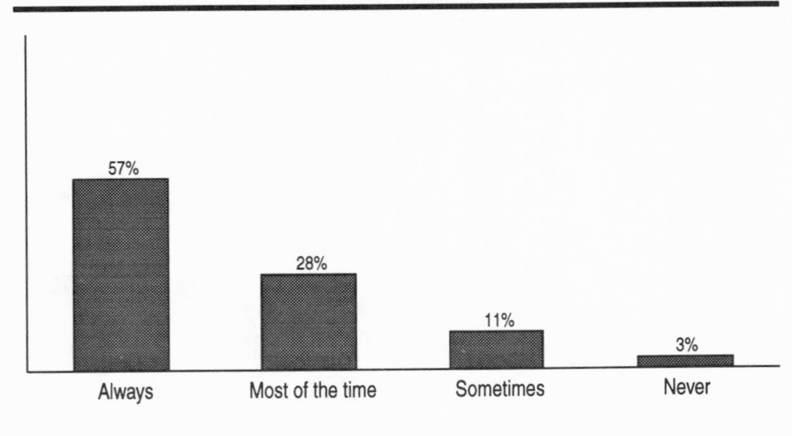

FIGURE 5.4

Parents' supportiveness during tough times. Just as many of our teens report that they and their parents communicate well, many also testify that their parents are supportive during tough times, a vital way to help teens take God seriously. Teens who feel their parents support them during crises have a more positive view of God than other teens. As shown in Figure 5.4, only three percent of teens who feel unsupported by their parents view God positively, compared to 57% who do feel supported. As parents, we cannot save our teenagers from all trauma, but if we explicitly support them when they face difficult situations they are *19 times more likely* to believe that God is important!

Setting limits and boundaries. While teens do need both a degree of personal autonomy and the support of their parents, they also need boundaries. From personal experience and through our research we are convinced these boundaries should be fair, consistent, and loving.

When we asked teens about their parents' rules, we asked not only for descriptions of the rules themselves but also about the love and support behind the rules. Accordingly, we divided the families into four categories: authoritarian (many rules and little parental support), authoritative (many rules and much parental support), permissive (few rules and much parental support), and neglectful (few rules and little parental support).

As we reported in our two previous books, teens in authoritative families are generally the most sexually chaste and the least likely to use alcohol and drugs. Conversely, teens in neglectful families are at the most risk in these areas. As Figure 5.5 illustrates, the same patterns occur regarding spiritual formation. We discovered that teens in authoritative families are the most likely both to take God seriously and to allow Christ to make a difference in their lives, while teens in neglectful families are the least likely to do so.

IMPORTANCE OF GOD AND PARENTING STYLES

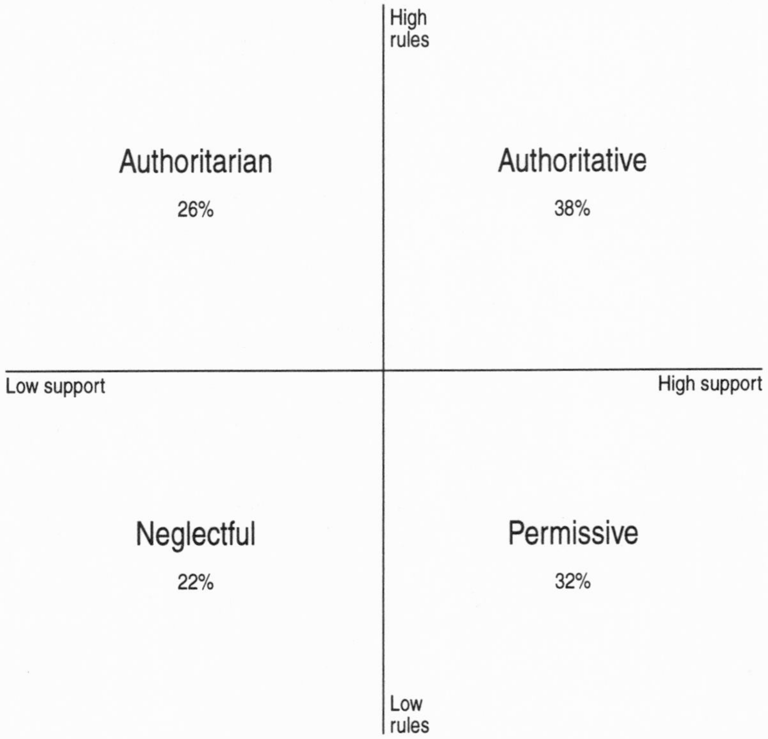

	Low support	High support
High rules	Authoritarian 26%	Authoritative 38%
Low rules	Neglectful 22%	Permissive 32%

FIGURE 5.5

All of our research shows that consistent, loving rules significantly complement spiritual formation. The more teens perceive a family rule as "fair" or "consistent," the more likely they are to grow spiritually. As Figure 5.6 reveals, teens who perceive exceptional fairness and consistency in their parents' rules are *25 times more likely* to view God seriously than teens who never perceive fairness and consistency in such boundaries. We can't help observing that parents do mirror divine values to their children. If parents are loving, steadfast, caring, and supportive, their offspring are much more likely to see God as important to their lives. Conversely, parents who are arbitrary, inconsistent, unconcerned, or indifferent are weighting their children down with a deadly millstone.

IMPORTANCE OF GOD AND PARENTING RULES AND LIMITS

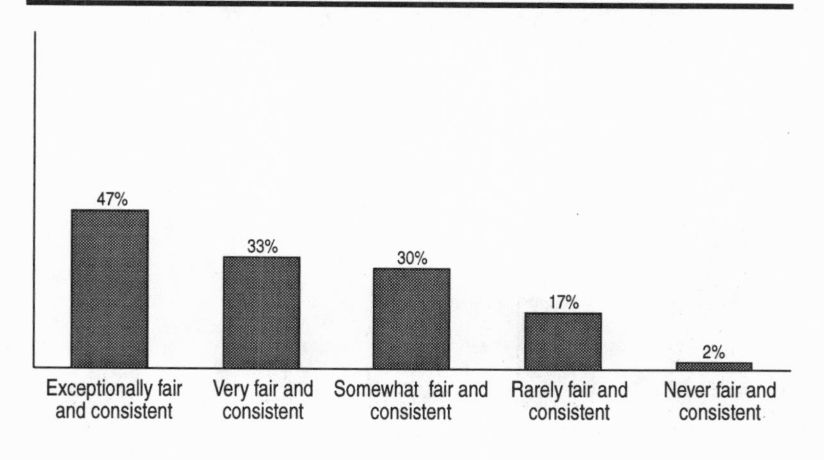

FIGURE 5.6

Parental spiritual leadership. Sixty-seven percent of the teens we surveyed report that their fathers have a serious faith in God; only 15% state that their fathers do not. Eighty-three percent of the same teens believe their mothers have a serious faith while only five percent believe their mothers lacked this quality.

As Figure 5.7 indicates, in order for teens to view their parents as deeply faithful, parents need to express their faith to their teens verbally. The children of parents who talk about God and spiritual issues a lot are over *five times more likely* to develop spiritually than the children of parents who do not talk about God. So it is important not only for parents to *have* a deep faith, but to *express* that faith to their children. The words of Deuteronomy exhort us all to share stories of our faith in God and his faithfulness to us: "Teach [these precepts] to your children, talking about them when you sit at home and when you walk along the road, when you lie down and when you get up" (11:19, NIV).

TAKING GOD SERIOUSLY AND PARENTAL TALKING ABOUT GOD

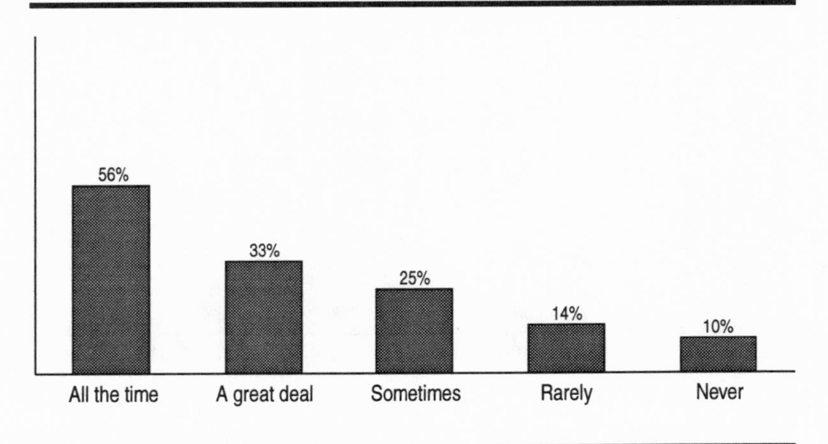

FIGURE 5.7

Focused attention from parents. To examine the amount of time Christian parents and adolescents spend together we asked the teens: "On average, how much time would you guess your father/mother spends giving you *focused attention* (listening and talking only to you, and making you feel special and important)?"

Nearly one-fifth of the teens indicate that their fathers spend less than fifteen minutes a week with them. That's only two minutes a day! Over one-fourth of the fathers spend three or more hours a week with their teens—about thirty minutes a day. And about one-third of mothers spend three or more hours per week giving their teens focused attention.

Our study clearly shows that the amount of time parents spend with their adolescents affects spiritual formation. As Figures 5.8 and 5.9 show, an increase in the amount of focused parental attention results in an increase in teens' viewing God as helpful. For example, the teen of a mother who focuses on him over five hours a week, rather than merely two or three, is 30% more likely to see God as helpful.

HELPFULNESS OF GOD AND TIME WITH MOM

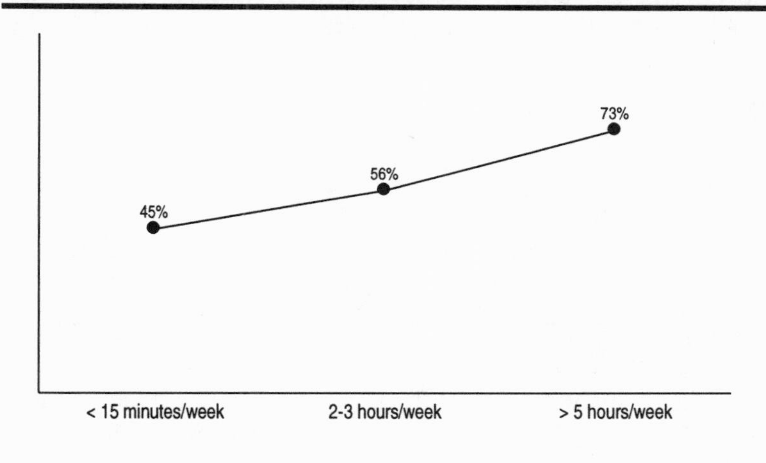

FIGURE 5.8

HELPFULNESS OF GOD AND TIME WITH DAD

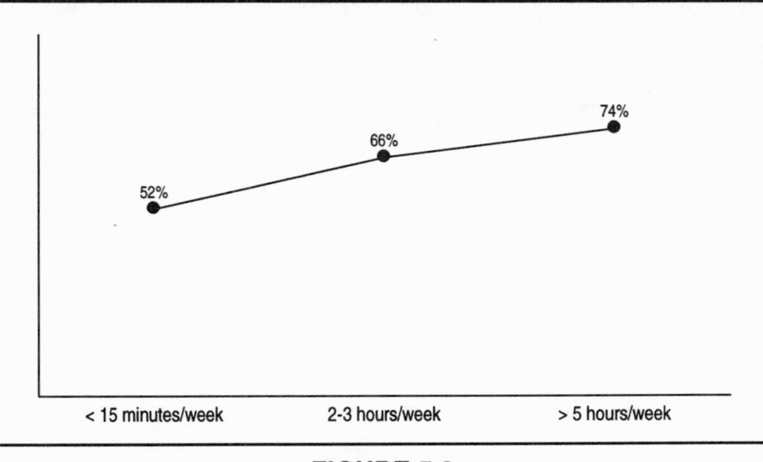

FIGURE 5.9

As we've noted before, teens who receive attention from Mom or Dad are much less likely to act out sexually and to use alcohol and drugs. Our teens are telling us of their brokenness and of their need for listening, talking, and the sharing of faith. It would be difficult to overstate how much teens' relationships with their parents affect their spirituality. As the information in this chapter demonstrates, teens desperately need their parents' attention, time, and care. This care includes loving yet firm boundaries concerning behavior and morality. Additionally, as our teens grow we must generously allow autonomy so that they can learn to make decisions and act morally on their own accord. Finally, as we balance setting limits and allowing certain liberties, perhaps the greatest gift we can offer our teens is our *presence*. When in crisis, our teens need affirmation. More than our constructive criticism or even our protection, teens need our willingness to stand beside them as they test their own actions and judgment. Just as our Father allows us to make painful mistakes, and yet still comforts us, so also we need to bless our adolescents by supporting and respecting their growth into adulthood.

Painful Family Memories. Seventy-one percent of the teens report childhood days filled with positive memories. Yet they do recall a variety of traumas from their younger years which are listed in Table 5.1.

CHILDHOOD DIFFICULTIES

1	**Death** of a family member or close friend
2	**Parental divorce** and subsequent remarriage
3	**Father's alcohol** use and abuse
4	Serious personal **injury** or **illness**
5	**Parental abuse,** whether physical, emotional or sexual
6	**Drug abuse** by an older sibling
7	**Poverty,** mainly due to failed marriages
8	**Emotional illness** of a family member
9	**Sexual acting out** of an older sibling
10	**Father under-involvement** due to time pressures at work

TABLE 5.1

As we analyzed how these events affect the teens' walk with God, we found that those who suffered traumatic experiences in their formative years generally have more difficulty accepting Christ. We are not asserting that those traumatized adolescents will never find a fulfilling relationship with Christ. Obviously, events such as the death of a family member or serious personal injury are beyond human control. But whenever possible these difficulties should be mitigated by special love and nurture.

Certainly, this is the case with sexual abuse. Although the sexual abuse of children occurs significantly less in Christian families than in the general population, it is still a problem for a small proportion of our adolescents (about 4% tell us they have experienced abuse by their fathers). Figure 5.10 shows this percentage and a breakdown of the actual levels of inappropriate behavior by the fathers.

SEXUAL ABUSE BY FATHER

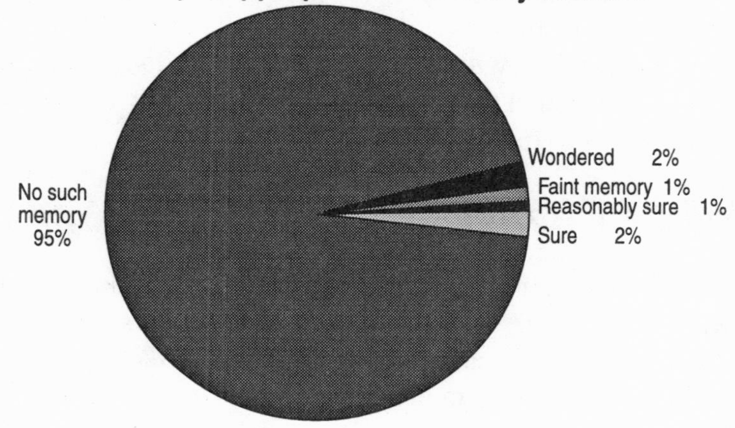

(Continued on next page)

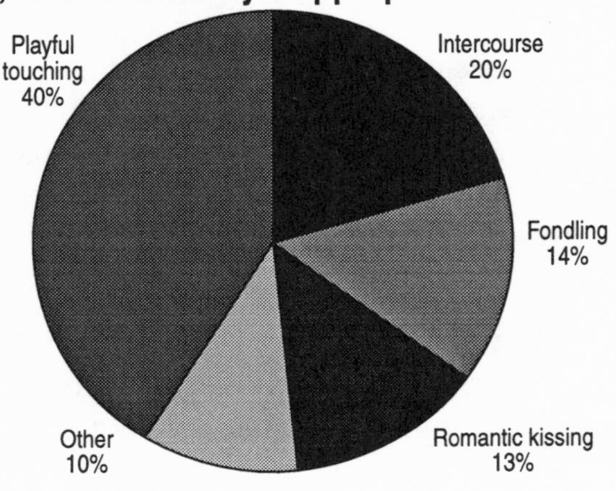

FIGURE 5.10

Though any degree of abuse is disturbing, it is estimated that "in the general population, from 15% to 45% of females and three to nine percent of all males have been sexually traumatized as children."[2] Although we believe child abuse occurs less within the community of God, there may be many Christian teens who have been sexually abused but are reluctant to report it.

What Changes Do Our Teens Want?

Significant insights in our study also come from the responses teens give when we asked what changes they would like to see in their parents. As we travel across the country, we consistently see parents riveted by the responses listed in Tables 5.2 and 5.3. These tables certainly reveal the desires of our teens' hearts.

DESIRED CHANGES IN MOTHER

1 **Open** — I wish she would be more open about her own past, especially her teen relationships with boyfriends, mother, etc.

2 **Loosen up** — I wish she would lighten up as I get older and allow me to make many of my own decisions

3 **Confidence in God** — I wish she trusted the Lord more to take care of me and not spend so much time worrying.

4 **Let go** — I wish she wasn't holding on so tightly to me and would realize that the older I get the less I need her rules.

5 **Energetic** — I wish she weren't so tired at the end of each day and had time for me and my problems.

6 **Confidence in me** — I wish she would understand that I need privacy; she is too nosy.

7 **Moodiness** — I wish she weren't so moody and temperamental. I get tired of PMS.

8 **Music tolerance** — I wish she understood how important music is to me and not try to interfere with my musical tastes.

9 **Communicative** — I wish that she were easier to talk to and would spend more time listening to me than talking to me.

10 **Accepting** — I wish she could accept my friends and care more about what I think than about what her friends think.

TABLE 5.2

DESIRED CHANGES IN FATHER

1 **Availability** — I wish he could spend more time with me.

2 **Self-control** — I wish he could get a grip on his anger and temper outbursts.

3 **God-oriented** — I wish he would care about spiritual matters more than his career

4 **Vulnerability** — I wish he could be more honest about his past and also his present. It would make us closer.

5 **Accepting of me as a person** — I wish he would like me for who I am and not just what I can do athletically, etc.

6 **Genuine** — I wish he wouldn't be so superficial when it comes to talking about topics like sexuality and alcohol or drug use.

7 **Boldness with faith commitment** — I wish he were not so embarassed to talk openly about his own Christian commitment.

8 **Confidence in God and me** — I wish he were more confident about my making good decisions and God's taking care of me.

9 **Respectful** — I wish he would listen first to my opinions and needs before making up his mind or jumping to conclusions.

10 **Approachable** — I wish he could make me feel safe and comfortable in sharing my real struggles with him.

TABLE 5.3

At this point it might be good to put this book down, to reflect, pray, and seek God's wisdom, and even be so bold as to ask the teens closest to you to comment on how well *you* display these traits.

A Concluding Note about Families

Let us say again that we are not degrading the need for psychologists or for treatment of mental or emotional problems. But our focus must first be Bible-centered. Even after counseling, therapy, and still more treatment, problems will remain. We agree with Charles Siburt:

> I'm for prevention. I'm for heading off as much hell as possible on this earth. But after you have done everything, in our flesh and in our fleshy families "dwelleth no good thing." The Bible calls that "no good thing" *sin*, not "dysfunction."

The church should reassert that no perfection or ideal exists while we or our families are in the flesh. Family members will always war against each other and hurt each other to some extent. Families still can cry out with Paul, "Oh, wretched *family* that we are, who shall deliver *us* from the body of this death?" The goal is not to look like a sentimental Norman Rockwell portrait, but to be families deeply faithful and committed to God. And through relationship with him, God will show us how to live in peace and true health. Despite our sin, our pain, and our hurting each other, he will deliver us. We may all shout, "Thanks be to God through Jesus Christ that there is now no condemnation for *families* that are in Christ Jesus our Lord . . . who walk not after the flesh but after the Spirit" (paraphrase, Romans 8:1,4).

[1] Charles Siburt, Portraits of God: Abilene Christian University's Youth and Family Conference, Feb. 1991.

[2] A. Browne and D. Finkelhor, "The Traumatic Impact of Child Sexual Abuse: A Conceptualization," *American Journal of Orthopsychiatry* 55.4 (1990): 530-541.

6

"Abiding Presence:" The Holy Spirit and Teen Spirituality

Beyond the sacred page, I seek Thee, Lord. My spirit pants for Thee, O Living Word. —Mary Ann Lathbury

For you did not receive a spirit of slavery to fall back into fear, but you have received a spirit of adoption. When we cry, 'Abba! Father!' it is that very Spirit bearing witness with our spirit that we are children of God. . . . —Romans 8:15

We may ignore, but we can nowhere evade, the presence of God. The world is crowded with Him. He walks everywhere incognito. And the incognito is not always hard to penetrate. The real labor is to remember, to attend. —C. S. Lewis

---

Americans, in great numbers, are rediscovering the spiritual life. All over the land, people are turning to prayer, the spiritual disciplines, Bible study, and devotional literature. In the words of church historian Martin Marty, "Spirituality is back, almost with a vengeance."

Richard Foster, the author of contemporary classics *Celebration of Discipline* and *Prayer*, says that America is undergoing "a quiet revolution." Some are comparing it to the Great Awakening, a spirit of revival that swept the country in the early eighteenth century.[1] Eugene Peterson, popular author of several books on spirituality and translator of *The Message*, reports a "ground swell of recognition spreading through our culture that all life is at root spiritual; that everything we see is formed and sustained by what we cannot see."[2]

This ground swell is evident in many ways. Churches are launching round-the-clock prayer sessions for missions. Retreat centers are booked two years in advance. Colleges and seminaries are creating new courses in spirituality. Books on spirituality now outsell old favorites on recovery and self-help. According to *Books in Print* there are nearly 2,000 titles on prayer, meditation, and spiritual growth—more than three times the number of books devoted to sexual intimacy.[3]

Throughout this book we have suggested that our children are susceptible to the spiritual, moral, and social forces sweeping our country. When it comes to matters of spirituality—and specifically to attitudes about the Holy Spirit—we find our young people mirror these contemporary trends. Like many of their peers, they are spiritually hungry and searching. They are searching for a true spirituality, a life connected to the holy, transcendent God.

Our children's view of the Holy Spirit can be most succinctly captured in three brief statements: they believe; they are receptive; they are confused. We will attempt to outline our findings on what our adolescents think, according to these three propositions.

Neither Rationalist nor Charismatic

First, we must recognize that our teens believe firmly in the Holy Spirit, with few exceptions. They view the Holy Spirit positively, and they believe in his present-day working in the world and personal involvement in their lives. This position certainly deviates from the popular myth that people in the Church of Christ are phobic about the Holy Spirit. Generally, we find our youth open and receptive to the Spirit.

While embracing the reality of the Spirit, our teens at the same time resist extreme positions on the subject. Respondents generally chart a middle way between two extremes; those who deny the Spirit's power and present activity in the world today, and those who argue for dramatic, charismatic manifestations. Most of our teens, as the charts later in this chapter will show, are quite accepting of a genuine power that moves and works among them. One student writes, "The Holy Spirit has power far beyond what my mind can comprehend." A college student cajoles the church for its apparent reluctance to embrace the Spirit more fully: "Why are we so afraid? Come on, we are all big people!" Another comments, "I have experienced first-hand his interceding, strengthening, and empowering." And another, "Don't they realize that they are sweeping not only our hearts, but our very lives under the rug when they are silent on the power of the Holy Spirit?"

A few openly rebel against the theological boundaries that our tradition has placed on the Spirit. A senior-high teen writes, "People have tried to tell me that the Holy Spirit does not act now in the same way that he did in the first century. I believe, however, that the Lord can do whatever he pleases, whether we like it or not." Another chides, "Most noncharismatic Christians tend to completely ignore the Holy Spirit—a little bit over-reactive, wouldn't you say?"

Yet most of our teens are reluctant to embrace the mystical or the supernatural. Uneasy about the claims of charismatics, they want a rational check on extreme religious enthusiasm. One junior-high student shrewdly asks, "How am I to know when it is the Holy Spirit, and when it's me working?" Another questions, "Does the Holy Spirit work miracles, or do I just not have enough faith?" Or, "If the Holy Spirit is working in my life, then is there ever such a thing as coincidence?" Others reflect a sadness at the absence of spiritual feeling: "How come when I pray, I don't feel his presence?" (In a culture dedicated to feeling and dramatic personal experience, this question is a big one for many.)

Some are either confused—or agnostic—about the Holy Spirit. "Why does this seem to be such an important subject and [yet] there is so much confusion among leaders?" A junior-high youth laments, "Why is all this stuff so confusing?" A senior-high Christian concurs, "I'm totally confused. I just don't understand any of this!" Many students express doubts, not about the Spirit's existence, but about his availability and willingness to help them with their struggles. "Why doesn't he help me with sexual temptation, illnesses, and bad behavior? What does he do in my life? How does he work in my life?" They ask these questions in many ways.

The rationalist mindset shines through in some cases. "How could [the Holy Spirit] help with two or more prayers at the same time?" one inquiring mind asks. Some are downright dismissive: "In my life there is God, Jesus, others, and me. The Holy Spirit does not play any role that I can see."

But the most striking thing about our adolescents' comments on the Holy Spirit is their sincerity, their longing for the truth of the matter, and their quest for balance. They don't want polemic or self-serving justifications. They want Scripture. One college student complains, "I have asked so many questions, and everywhere I have gone I have received conflicting answers without much Scripture to back up what they believe." Another writes, "My home church never mentions the Holy Spirit because they are fearful of being branded as a 'radical' church. In my opinion, fear is of the devil!" One college student asks for balance: "In the Church of Christ, it's simply been a taboo subject for nearly 100 years. We have reacted to the Pentecostal movement in the right ditch, and by reacting, we fall into the other ditch. I guess I'm not impressed with either place." This last comment causes us to offer this generalization: Overwhelmingly, our teens occupy a centrist position on the Holy Spirit.

Holy Spirit: Alive and Near at Hand

In order to understand our teens' opinions about the Holy Spirit, we asked them to respond to six questions concerning the Holy Spirit. The questions were designed to indicate if the teens tended toward a rationalist/analytical view of the Spirit or a more charismatic/affective view. Using a five-point scale, respondents indicated where on the continuum they would place themselves. Quite significantly, our teens clustered near the middle on each question. In other words, our children generally reject extreme rationalist *and* extreme charismatic positions. Our children believe that God's Spirit is alive and at work in the world, touching us, shaping us, and changing us quietly from within. But radical, dramatic, and sensational activities attributed to the Holy Spirit, they believe, are suspect (see the appendix at the conclusion of this chapter).

Our respondents describe a number of ways in which the Holy Spirit works today. They see him as making confession possible. He pours love in their hearts. He guides and gives counsel. He reassures them that they are his children when their hearts cause them to doubt. He guarantees eternal salvation.

Our children's views are not far different from those of church leaders, it turns out. We surveyed preachers and elders and found that in some cases the church leaders even attribute *more* influence and power to the Spirit than do our children. Every one of the preachers surveyed, for example, agreed that the Holy Spirit pours God's love into our hearts; 93% of the elders concurred, followed by 91% of college Christians, and 83% of high-schoolers. On the other hand, more than twice as many high-school respondents (10%) believe the Spirit has worked a miracle in their lives compared to preachers (4%) or elders (4%). Specifically, these are the percentages of high-schoolers who respectively agree with these statements:

In my experience the Holy Spirit has . . .

- 83%—poured the love of God into my heart.
- 76%—given me the power to confess verbally that Jesus is Lord.
- 75%—been my own personal counselor who lives within me.
- 75%—interpreted my heart to God when I didn't have to words to express myself.
- 73%—reassured me that I am a child of God when I began to doubt.
- 69%—convicted me of sin by making me feel guilty.

- 68%—given me special gifts (like wisdom, faith, mercy, and knowledge) to encourage and build up the church.
- 67%—guaranteed me that I will have eternal life now and forever.
- 63%—given me the power to avoid sexual immorality.
- 51%—kept me from having a divisive and quarrelsome spirit.
- 40%—made available to believers the same power that raised Jesus from the dead.
- 32%—been able to know the inner thoughts of God and shared them with me.
- 21%—caused me to believe in such a way that at times others thought I was crazy or strange.
- 12%—enabled me to speak in tongues, prophesy, and/or distinguish between the spirits.
- 10%—enabled me to do miraculous things such as healing, casting out demons, and/or other miraculous signs and wonders through the name of the Holy Spirit.

We may conclude a number of things in the light of our survey. First, our teens do feel empowered by the Holy Spirit, though their responsiveness to the Spirit varies considerably, according to the style and emphasis of the local congregation and the attitude of their parents. Confusion and uncertainty about the Spirit's nature and work, though not universal, is widespread. Our children are not the rationalists that their parents or grandparents allegedly were, but they seem unsure what precisely they should believe about the Spirit. They want balanced, honest, fair, biblical instruction.

We suggest that church leaders and teachers provide ample instructions, advice, and counsel about the meaning of God's Spirit. We offer the following suggestions as beginning points.

Return to the Scriptures. Many of our children are, by their own admission, illiterate about the Holy Spirit. Some don't believe in him at all. Others, through an obvious lack of instruction, have virtually made him a separate deity. One student reflects a kind of nascent tri-theism when he asks, "What is the Holy Spirit's rank among God and Jesus?"

Dr. Lynn Anderson reminds us of the critical importance of the Holy Spirit in the Bible:

> Everybody who is a Christian has been "double" baptized. John 3:5 says that "except a man be born of water *and* the Spirit, he cannot enter the kingdom of heaven." The expression of baptism in the Spirit appears seven times: four times in the Gospels, twice in Acts, and once in 1 Corinthians 12:13. And in every one of those situations in the Gospels, the same thing is being discussed . . .
>
> In Luke 4 John the Baptist says, "I baptize you in water, but one is coming after me whose shoes I am not worthy to unloose. He will baptize you with the Holy Spirit and with fire." That same expression is repeated in Matthew, Mark, and John. So this is not some strange outpouring. Paul says in Ephesians 4 that there is one baptism, but that one baptism includes two elements. Every person who is baptized is baptized in water and the Spirit . . .
>
> Every person who becomes a Christian is overwhelmed and immersed in the Spirit. This is another way of saying that they are indwelt, or the Holy Spirit comes to live in them. Now if we are overwhelmed by the Spirit or if the Spirit comes to

> live within us, what is the evidence of it? How do we know that? First, we know that because God said so and God doesn't break his promises. "If you repent and are baptized you will receive the gift of the Holy Spirit." He will baptize you with the Holy Spirit. But we also know that the Holy Spirit dwells in us and helps with the practical issues of life.[4]

Of course, excellent balanced, informed, theological treatments of the subject are widely available.[5] While this chapter is not a place to present a full theology of the Holy Spirit, we feel the need to say briefly that instruction about the Spirit must be more balanced and fully connected to the rest of our theology. Our teaching should lead us, always, to relate the Spirit's ministry to Jesus and the Father. After all, the Holy Spirit is also the Spirit of Christ (2 Corinthians 3:17), the continuing presence of Jesus on the earth (John 14:18-28). A good test of teaching on the Holy Spirit is this, "Does it lead us back to Jesus Christ?" (See 1 Corinthians 12:1-3).

Living with the Mystery

In our discussions of the Spirit, we must beware of claiming to know more than we in fact know. Our understanding of God's sovereignty and power should cause us to speak humbly and circumspectly on this topic, as with all topics related to the deity. One of our respondents confesses freely, "I don't know the whole story." All of us can make that confession. In instructing Nicodemus, Jesus instructs us all when he says, "The wind [or Spirit] blows where it chooses, and you hear the sound of it, but you do not know where it comes from or where it goes. So it is with everyone who is born of the Spirit" (John 3:8, NRSV). Many of our children are dissatisfied because they want a rational, comprehensible explanation of the Spirit's work. One college student complains, "He is just not as concrete and tangible to me as I would like for him to be." But, then, if the Spirit is spirit, why should he be concrete and tangible? This may be a perfect occasion to teach against that form of idolatry which demands a visible, sensible deity.

David Wolpe reminds us: "A tragedy of humanity in our time is the certainty that what we see is what alone exists, what we create is alone worthy. . . .We suffer the peculiar blindness of those who see only the visible."[6] That the Holy Spirit is incomprehensible should not disturb us. It should lead us to exuberant praise and humble thanksgiving. The Holy Spirit will always transcend our knowing, and that is good. Our children, like all of us, need a majestic, mysterious God who surpasses their own knowledge. Emily Dickinson once wrote, "It is true that the unknown is the largest need of the intellect, though for it, no one thinks to thank God."[7] We must learn to appreciate the mystery of a God who condescends to our level, who lives in our hearts, and who prompts us to loving service.

Teaching His Presence

A pressing need of our time, which profoundly affects our children, is the longing to experience the divine presence. This hope is not unique to our age. One finds it poignantly illustrated in the Bible. In Exodus 33, for example, Moses rather bluntly refuses to lead the recalcitrant Israelites to the Promised Land until he knows who will go with him. Moses demands of God, "Show me your ways, so that I may know you and find favor in your sight" (NRSV). God reassures Moses, "My presence will go with you, and I will give you rest." But Moses is not satisfied. He asks for a dramatic demonstration of the divine presence. Moses pleads, "Show me your glory, I pray." Then God warns Moses that he doesn't know what he is asking for: "You cannot see my face; for no one shall see me and live." The Lord then conceals Moses in a cleft of a rock, and God covers Moses with his hand while his glory passes by. God says, "I will cover you with my hand until I have passed by; then I will take away my hand, and you shall see my back, but my face shall not be seen." Moses does not see the face of God; he only sees God's back and the place where God has been. There is a lesson in this extraordinary experience. Like Moses, we long for the full encounter with God, but such meetings are not to be had. Traces and glimpses, perhaps. As T. S. Eliot explains in *Murder in the Cathedral*,

"Only in retrospection, selection, / We say, that was the day. / Only in retrospection does the eternal design appear."[8]

This longing to experience God in some way has always been with God's people. "Show us your glory"—it was a longing of Christians in the last century when John E. Bode wrote so eloquently:

O let me feel Thee near me:
The world is ever near;
I see the sights that dazzle,
The tempting sounds I hear;
My foes are ever near me,
Around me and within;
But, Jesus, draw Thou nearer,
And shield my soul from sin.

Thomas O. Chisholm in "Be With Me, Lord" perfectly summarizes the hope of our parents:

Be with me, Lord! No other gift or blessing
Thou couldst bestow could with this one compare—

A constant sense of Thy abiding presence,
Where'er I am, to feel that Thou art near.

Though the petition is expressed in terms of the Spirit's immanence, rather than Jesus' or the Father's nearness, our children are calling for the same intimacy with the divine:

> Rushing wind blow through me
> With your tender breeze
> Search out the depths of my heart
> Like a fire burn through me
> Here on my knees
> Consume every dark hidden part.

Opportunity and Danger

The expectation of intimacy is understandable, universal, and biblical, but it is also potentially disillusioning and dangerous. There are ways open to us to experience God's presence, and there are ways that are closed to us. Not every faithful follower gets what he wants, the way he wants it. If we do not teach this truth clearly to our children, we set them up for bitter disappointment when they experience the silence of God. Moses got something from God, but he didn't get what he asked for. For a time, Job was disappointed, as was Jeremiah, Paul, and even Jesus. God is no Oriental genie, duty-bound to respond to our slightest requests. God's presence and apparent absence are much more complicated than our religious talk implies. We must give our children a better theology of the Spirit. Ecstatic encounters with God are not necessarily everyday affairs. Often, only in retrospect can we know where God has been.

As T. S. Eliot points out, sometimes the divine comes only in snatches—a wink, a glimpse, a whisper. And there may be long periods of dryness, in which we cry, "Where are you, God?" This painful questioning often begins early in our children's lives. We must be ready to cope with feelings of alienation and abandonment. Our children wonder: "How come when I pray I don't feel his presence?" "I believe all these things about the Holy Spirit, but why do I not feel him?" Our children need counselors who can help them see that the cry of dereliction (as in Psalm 22) is also a cry of faith. Henri Nouwen describes a central mission of every youth counselor and parent: "Ministry is the spiritual act of seeing and helping others see the face of a loving God even where nothing but darkness seems to be present."[9]

We need to think through the issue of divine presence and absence. Our children may not care to digest a lot of subtle theology about the Holy Spirit, but their questions tell us that it is of primary importance to them to know if he is *with them*, and, if so, *how*. Many of them have been led to define the Spirit's presence very simplistically, according to their feelings. ("I feel good" = "God is near"; "I feel depressed" = "God is absent.") We need to introduce them to a God who is so great, so loyal and trustworthy, that he transcends the feelings of their hearts (1 John 3:19-20). They must learn to trust his promises even when their senses betray them. And they must learn that obedience must come whether the feelings are there or not. In the words of Bonhoeffer: "Only he who believes is obedient, and only he who is obedient believes."[10]

Our children also need a theology of the Spirit that enables them to rise above the petty egocentrism of the Corinthians, who wanted spiritual gifts for selfish ends and personal glory. The blessings of the Spirit are dealt according to his sovereign will, "individually as the Spirit chooses" (1 Corinthians 12:11). He is under no obligation to give us what we want. The Spirit's goal is to build up the *whole* body of Christ, not to satisfy individuals' wish lists. Gifts are for the common good of the community of faith.

Ultimately, an appreciation for the Spirit will lead to spirituality—that is, the disciplines of living for God each day. In our research we discovered that the more teens engage in the spiritual disciplines, the more likely they will value the Holy Spirit (see Chapters Four and Nine).

Junk Food or Veggies?

Like hymn writer Mary Ann Lathbury, our children pant for the God who dwells both in Scripture and "beyond the sacred page." Members of the post-Baby Boom generation know there's something wrong with hedonism: "We are surprised to find ourselves lonely behind the wheel of a BMW or bored nearly to death as we advance from one prestigious job to another. And then, one by one, a few people begin to realize that getting more and doing more only makes the sickness worse."[11] The realization that the secular society can't deliver on its promises began as a trickle, but it has reached flood stage. Because of this, there is today great openness to the spiritual life. Yet there are many dangers in the search; many false spirits are abroad. Our children will be tempted to taste many false spiritualities—shamanism, pantheism, and Zen Buddhism, to name a few. Or they will encounter "secular" spiritualities which encourage a kind of vague love of wonder in nature, which leaves the God of Scripture out of the picture. How should we respond? Eugene Peterson offers some excellent concluding advice.

First, he says, "Discover what the Bible says about spirituality and immerse yourself in it."[12] He explains: "The Scriptural revelation is not only authoritative for what we believe about God and the way we behave with each other, but also for shaping and maturing our very souls, our *being*, in response to God." The best check on extremes in spirituality is a solid knowledge of the Word of God.

Second, he advises us to reject a spirituality that does not require a commitment to the community of faith. Many people on a spiritual quest today see it as an easy, "no-strings-attached" alternative to church. A spirituality without commitment to others is false. Peterson argues: "Personal commitment to the God personally revealed in Jesus is at the heart of spirituality. . . . Single-minded, persevering faithfulness confirms the authenticity of our spirituality." He adds that the spiritual giants of the past—Augustine, Calvin, and Bunyan—didn't flit. *"They stayed."*

Third, he invites us to learn about spirituality from many people and traditions. Our spiritual traditions go back four thousand years. Friends across town, around the world, or in previous centuries have much to teach us about the spiritual life.

Fourth, Peterson encourages us to return home and learn from the spirituality of our own tradition. He wisely warns us that there is a tendency to feel deprived by our own religious heritage:

> We suspect we were not provided our rightful heritage by our church or pastor or family, that we were not guided and nurtured in the ways of robust holiness . . . Angry over our impoverishment, we cannot help noticing churches or movements that look better.

Dr. B. J. Leonard, Chair of Samford University's Department of Religion and Philosophy, once asked this penetrating question in a seminar for scholars in Churches of Christ: "What is the nature of spirituality in Churches of Christ?" Many people would be surprised to know that there is a "Restoration spirituality," yet there most certainly is one. Unfortunately, though, it has been sadly neglected. It is high time we rediscovered our own spiritual heritage. The evidence of it lies all about us, for example, in the fervent hymns that have shaped our worship and our imaginations. It has often been remarked that our hymns have often conveyed a much healthier and richer theology than have our sermons. We would add that the hymns of Bernard of Clairvaux, Adelaide Pollard, Fannie J. Crosby, Charles Wesley, Thomas O. Chisholm, Tillit S. Teddlie, and a hundred others, reveal our true spirituality.

Our tradition is broader, richer, and deeper than many realize. We have never been very far from the wisdom of Thomas à Kempis, John Wesley, or C. S. Lewis.[13] As Leonard Allen has eloquently shown in his recent book *Distant Voices*, we have had our spiritual giants, like Dr. Robert Richardson, whose moving meditations at the Lord's table in Alexander Campbell's home church were widely published and greatly admired by thousands in the Restoration tradition. Richardson was a voice from the wilderness at times, when our movement turned polemical and cerebral.

> Too many people, he wrote, 'are ready to argue, debate, discuss, at all times, . . . and will spend hours in the earnest defense of their favorite theories,' but they will not spend five minutes meditating 'upon the character, the sayings, and perfections of Christ, or upon their own inward spiritual state.'[14]

Our spiritual tradition is also available to us through some of our finest preachers who, transcending polemic, envisioned the glorious grace of God. Professor Michael Casey of Pepperdine University, among others, is engaged in a project to help us rediscover the loving, peaceful, and spiritual messages of preachers like T. B. Larimore and K. C. Moser. Our spiritual heritage is still also visible through men like J. N. Armstrong whose labor at Cordell (Oklahoma) Christian College in the early twentieth century left a spiritual imprint on many of the early personalities at Harding University and Oklahoma Christian University.[15]

Rich new veins of Restoration spirituality are just waiting to be unearthed and restored to all of us. A great portion of our spiritual heritage resides with our mothers and grandmothers—how they prayed, how they taught their children the gospel, how they faced grueling hardships and disappointments. The time must soon come when we will invite our great women of faith to show us how they have met and communed with their God. We have a great spiritual heritage, and it must be passed on to our children.

Finally, Peterson encourages us to seek out mature teachers and guides. Knowing God means facing deep valleys as well as awesome peaks. The spiritually mature can help us do that. Peterson advises:

> There are many holy friends and pastors, teachers and...brothers and sisters among us. But they do not always advertise themselves. Seek them out. Cultivate their company either in person or through books. Because the appetite for God is easily manipulated into a consumer activity, we need these wise, sane friends as guides and companions.

There is great hunger among our youth today. But as Martin Marty warns, we must choose between Twinkies and broccoli. We must help our young locate and experience the real thing through Bible study, prayer, the disciplines, and a full life in the church. If we do these things, they will have a full spiritual life. It will be real. And it will last.

---

[1] Timothy Jones, "Great Awakenings," *Christianity Today* 8 Nov. 1993: 23.

[2] Eugene Peterson, "Spirit Quest," *Christianity Today* 8 Nov. 1993: 27.

[3] Jones, 23.

[4] Lynn Anderson, His Boundless Spirit: Abilene Christian University's Youth and Family Conference, Feb. 1993.

[5] See, for example: Frederick D. Bruner, *A Theology of the Holy Spirit* (Grand Rapids: Eerdmans, 1970); E. Earle Ellis, *Pauline Theology, Ministry and Society* (Grand Rapids: Eerdmans, 1989); Jürgen Moltmann, *The Church in the Power of the Spirit* Trans. Margaret Kohl (New York: Harper and Row, 1977); C. F. D. Moule, *The Holy Spirit* (London: A. R. Mowbray, 1978); John R. W. Stott, *The Baptism and Fullness of the Holy Spirit* (Downers Grove, Ill.: InterVarsity, 1964). We would further recommend a lecture series like John Allen Chalk's, "Like a Rushing Wind: The Holy Spirit in the Bible and in Our Lives."

[6] David J. Wolpe, *The Healer of Shattered Hearts: A Jewish View of God* (New York: Penguin, 1990) 18.

[7] Robert N. Linscott, ed., *Selected Poems and Letters of Emily Dickinson* (New York: Doubleday, 1959) 307.

[8] T. S. Eliot, *Murder in the Cathedral* (San Diego: Harcourt Brace Jovanovich, 1935) 57.

[9] Henri Nouwen, *Seeds of Hope* (New York: Bantam Books, 1989) 76.

[10] Dietrich Bonhoeffer, *The Cost of Discipleship* (New York: Macmillan, 1959) 69.

[11] Peterson, 28.

[12] The following points are based upon Peterson, 29-30.

[13] The popularity of writers like Max Lucado illustrates, implicitly, a pre-existing, congenial spiritual tradition in Churches of Christ.

[14] C. Leonard Allen, *Distant Voices: Discovering a Forgotten Past for a Changing Church* (Abilene: ACU Press, 1993) 65. See especially Chapter Nine, "Room for the Spirit," and Chapter Eleven, "Holy Mysteries."

[15] See Norman Parks, *Cordell's Christian College: A History* (Cordell, OK: Fourth and College Church of Christ, [1994]).

APPENDIX

ADOLESCENT VIEWS OF THE NATURE OF THE HOLY SPIRIT

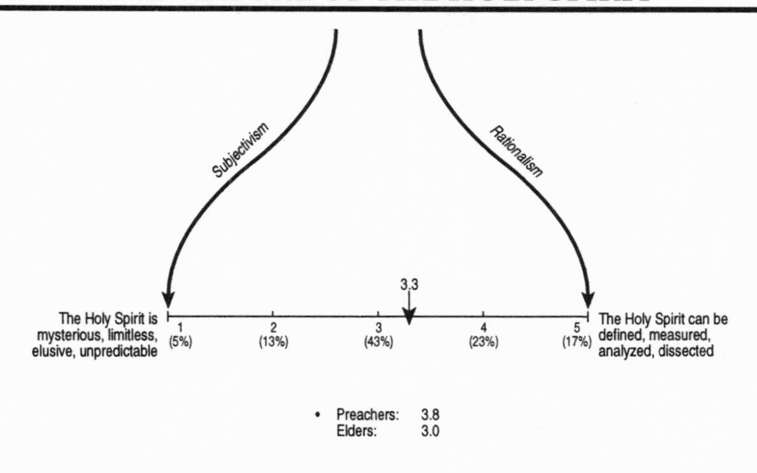

FIGURE 6.1

ADOLESCENT VIEWS OF THE METHODOLOGY OF THE HOLY SPIRIT

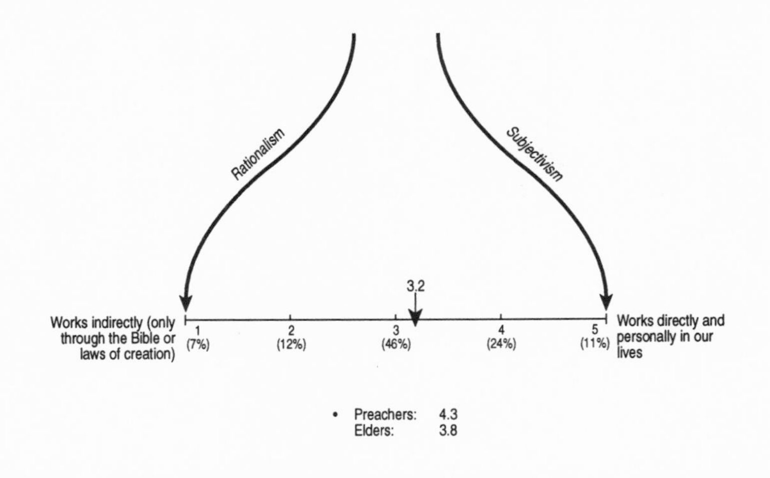

FIGURE 6.2

ADOLESCENT VIEWS OF THE OPERATION OF THE HOLY SPIRIT

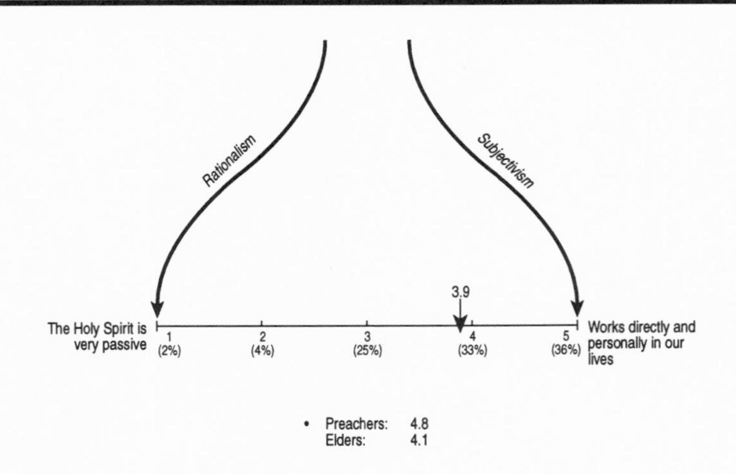

FIGURE 6.3

ADOLESCENT VIEWS OF THE POWER OF THE HOLY SPIRIT IN CONVERSION

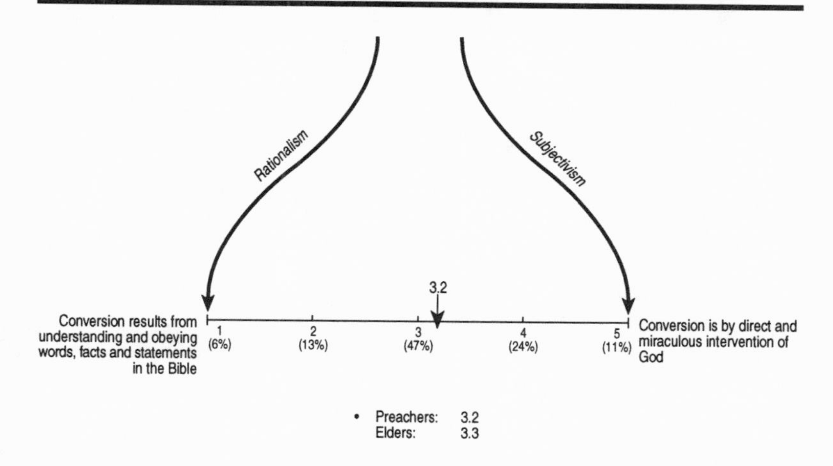

FIGURE 6.4

ADOLESCENT VIEWS OF THE PROCESS OF THE HOLY SPIRIT

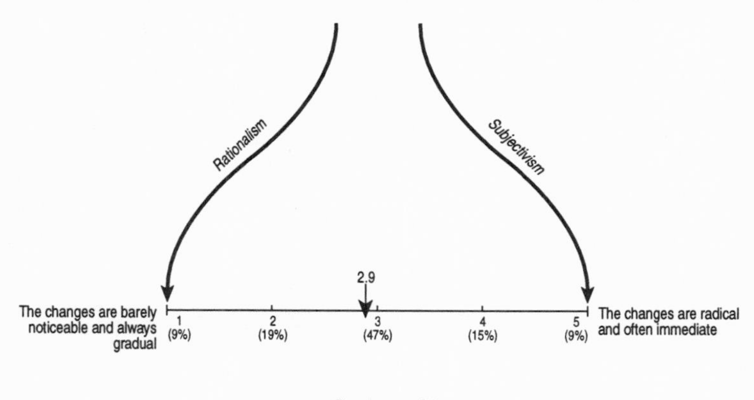

FIGURE 6.5

7

Baptism, Family Rituals, and The Life of Faith

There is nothing so secular that it cannot be sacred, and that is one of the deepest messages of the Incarnation. —Madeleine L'Engle

Your baptism in Christ was not just washing you up for a fresh start. It also involved dressing you in an adult faith wardrobe — Christ's life, the fulfillment of God's original purpose. —Galatians 3:27, *The Message*

Life without memory is no life at all. . . . Our memory is our coherence, our reason, or feeling, even our action. Without it, we are nothing. . . . —Luis Buñuel

Why do some people make a commitment to the Christian faith and remain faithful through the years, while others lose their enthusiasm and drift away? Jesus' parable of the sower and the soils (Mark 4:1-8) provides some answers to the question. Some believers abandon the faith because of immaturity or a lack of readiness (no roots); others succumb to a hostile or seductive environment (trouble, persecution, the desire for things), or to the power of Satan (the cares of the world, the lure of wealth).

There are additional answers to this fundamental question found throughout Scripture. Our survey of adolescent attitudes about baptism and faith has caused us to go back to Scripture and the Christian tradition to consider once again what encourages spiritual fidelity. We believe this chapter on baptism and other ceremonies of faith will help us see that *how* converts are inducted into the family of God has something to say about their future commitments to Christ. We believe, additionally, that congregations and families can, through a variety of customs and traditions, enhance the spiritual commitment of their children.

In this chapter we describe the ways in which our children view their baptisms. They tell us why they were baptized, who most influenced them to make the decision, and if their lives changed afterward. We then offer several concrete recommendations for making the baptismal event even more meaningful. We conclude with some advice for "ritualizing" our children's lives so they can keep alive the memory of what God has done and is doing through them.

Before we proceed, however, we must consider a major stumbling block. We live in a culture that treats "rite" or ceremony in a contradictory way. One the one hand, our professed attitude toward ceremony is often indifference or hostility. To say that something is "just a ritual" is to consign it to the dustbin of irrelevance. One can quickly think of the "dead forms" of some church's liturgy that no longer make sense in a modern world. Thus, ritual is defined as "empty, hollow, pointless"—perhaps even "hypocritical." For many, ritual means "going through the motions" with heart or head disengaged. In such a cultural setting, even Christians talk as though ritual is inherently bad.

On the other hand, all of us practice—and, in fact, deeply value—rituals and ceremonies They are simply customary ways of doing things, whether these things are dubbed "sacred" or "secular." Whether it is reciting the Pledge of Allegiance in a school assembly or reading the 23rd Psalm at a funeral, nearly everyone knows that ritual can deeply engage the heart and mind. Rituals profoundly shape how we unite in matrimony, bury our dead, elect our leaders, and approach God in communal worship. Rituals govern how we meet strangers, how we address our peers, dress ourselves, dine at a restaurant, or behave at a football game. "Rites" govern all sorts of events in our lives—from what we do at Christmas and Thanksgiving to what we expect of each other at Sunday dinner. Marriage and family counselors are discovering that families with strong traditions tend to be more stable and better equipped to handle shocks that often devastate less ritualized families. Rituals, properly understood, never detract from meaningful living; instead, they enrich and fortify our lives.

Any Christian who wants to pass the Christian faith on to the next generation had better not be cavalier about rite and ceremony, for one of the functions of ritual is to help believers remember. "In memory resides the secret of redemption," the founder of Hasidism once taught his followers. Ritual is one of the most powerful means to keep memory alive. People without it suffer from spiritual amnesia. All the great forms of worship and celebration in the Bible (Passover, the Lord's Supper, and baptism, for example) are "memorials," intended to help us remember who we are, who God is, how we must live, where we have been, and where we are going.

This truth certainly helps us see why baptism was such a significant ritual in the apostolic churches. It marked the pagan convert's radical transition from the kingdom of darkness into the kingdom of light. The rite of baptism meant annihilation and rebirth, the end to one form of existence and the dramatic birth of another. It signaled the eviction of Satan from the human heart and the welcoming of the living Christ. It marked the end of one form of possession in order to make room for possession by God's own Spirit. It also was an unforgettable memorial, reminding the convert who had saved him, who had bought him, and who had entered him. And it reminded him of the ultimate goal of Christlikeness, to be shaped in the image of Jesus Christ.

In modern times, Restoration churches have attempted to preserve and promote the biblical, apostolic emphasis upon baptism as the premier event in the life of the believer. Partly because of a unique heritage—a militant biblicism blended with Reformation theology and frontier revivalism—Churches of Christ have continued to preach forcefully baptism's power to translate the individual, alien soul from the grip of evil into the ark of safety, the church, the body of Christ. The rhetoric of our sermons and our numerous writings on conversion loudly proclaim the centrality of baptism to the transformed life. Baptism, for us, is the fulcrum of faith. This pivotal event in the believer's salvation is synonymous with "conversion"—at once dramatic, radical, and complete.

However, when we interview our own baptized children, the picture is not quite so theatrical or climactic. While our teens overwhelmingly value their experience of immersion, they don't usually consider it in the dramatic terms our theological tradition holds up as normative. Our adolescents do take baptism quite seriously, yet they are not able to testify to an experience that supports our colorful rhetoric about dramatic change. We must consider why there is such a gap between our theology of dramatic baptismal change, and the fact of change that is comparatively subdued, incremental, and colorless.

First, let us consider what prompted our teens to be baptized. Of the baptized teens we surveyed, most indicate that they chose to be baptized as the result of a diligent, personal search rather than because of a spontaneous, peer-pressured decision. They do not see it as a quick fix to problems or a way merely to fit in. Interestingly, as Figure 7.1 shows, parents influence teens' thoughts about baptism most; their influence exceeds that of close friends, youth ministers, and other church leaders. And Figure 7.2 further demonstrates that many of our teens take baptism seriously.

GREATEST INFLUENCES ON BAPTISM

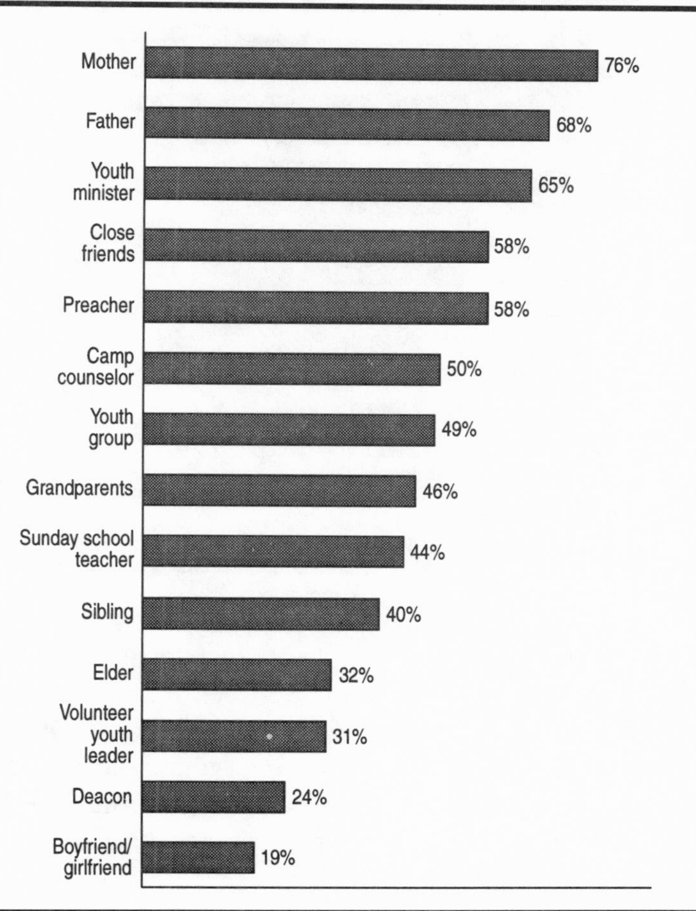

FIGURE 7.1

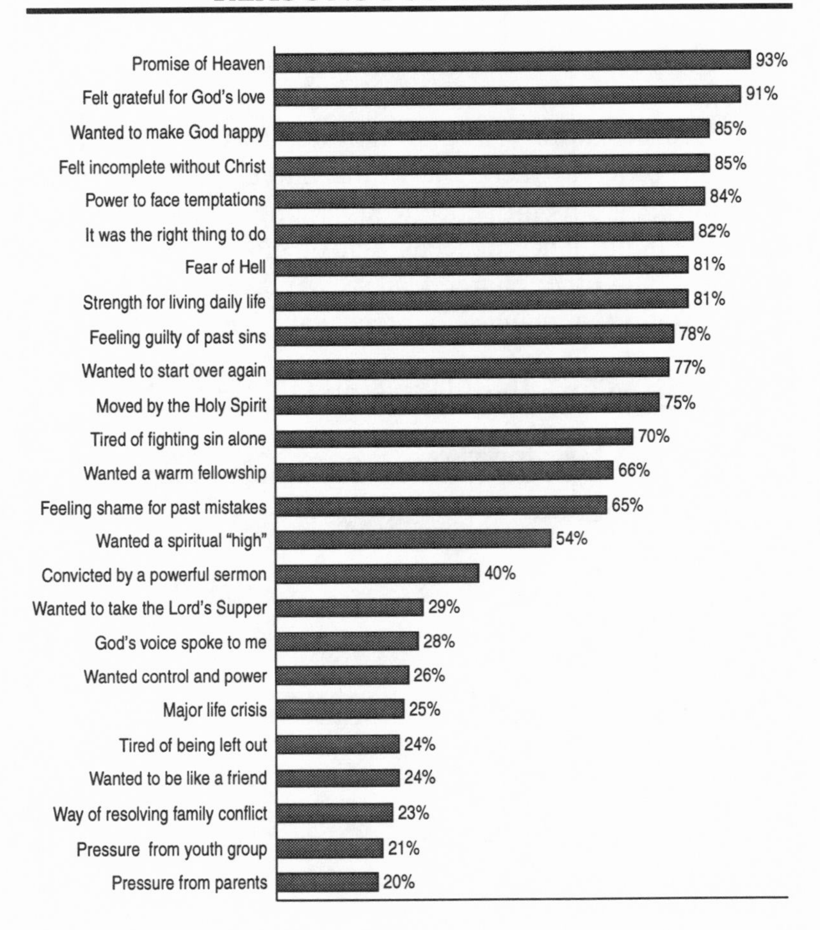

FIGURE 7.2

According to Pauline theology, baptism is meant to signal a major spiritual divide between a convert's fallen existence and his "new creation" in Christ. "So if anyone is in Christ, there is a new creation: everything old has passed away; see, everything has become new!" (2 Corinthians 5:17, NRSV). Our traditional teaching asserts that a conversion is a radical change, a U-turn from a former way of life. Yet, in fact, our baptized children reveal that there is a significant gap, or time lag, between the baptismal event and major behavioral changes. The teens were, on average, 12 years old when they were baptized. Yet our respondents do not report major changes in the months following their decision. In fact, baptism does not seem to make a significant difference in their attitudes or actions until they are 15 or 16.

We have found comparable patterns in the past. Previously we have reported that it is not until adolescents are 15 or 16 that we can locate significant correlations between teens' baptisms and factors like sexual behavior or use of alcohol and drugs. Likewise, as Figure 7.3 illustrates, only when teens reach 15 or 16 does baptism correlate to their responses about God's importance in their lives.

IMPORTANCE OF GOD AND BAPTISM AND AGE

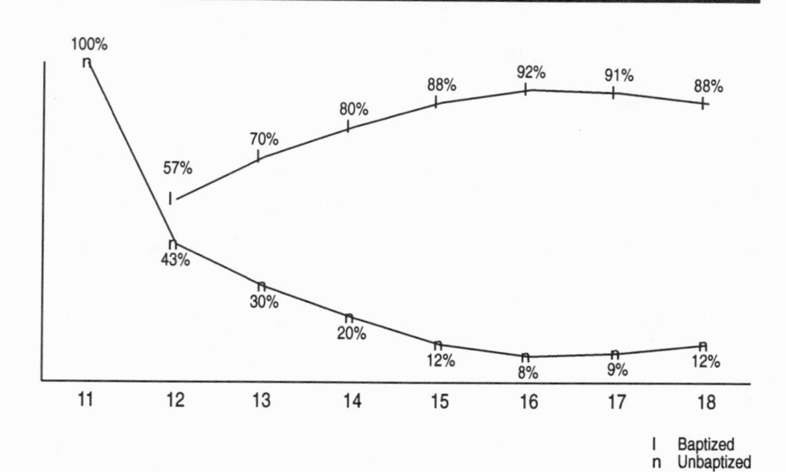

FIGURE 7.3

It appears that baptism is generally not as important to early teens immediately after it takes place as it later becomes. Why is this? One possible explanation is that older teens are better equipped to appreciate the need for God because their "sin consciousness" has been heightened through experience. Perhaps it is a developmental issue, that is, disciples may need to achieve a certain level of maturity before they can fully appreciate the meaning of the conversion experience. Though we do not know the causes of this lag between baptismal experience and its meaning for the adolescent believer, we believe many younger teens do not come to view their own baptisms as significant until a few years after it has occurred. This is not necessarily an argument against early baptisms, however. Nothing in our research suggests that those converted at the age of 12, for example, are less likely to remain faithful or ethically committed than those converted in their late teens. We are only arguing that older teens find a more immediate meaning in baptism.

The important insight from this data is what it says about the gap between the baptized and the unbaptized during the late teen years. We see little difference in spiritual outlook between baptized and unbaptized 12-year-olds. However, when we look at middle to late adolescence (10th, 11th, and 12th grades), there is a dramatic difference between the spiritual perception of those teens who are baptized and those who are not. For example, among unbaptized 16-year-olds, *only eight percent* view God as important to their lives! But among baptized 16-year-olds, 92% view God as important. In other words, the baptized 16-year-olds are more than *11 times more likely* to take God seriously. We are not accounting for this catastrophic difference—only reporting it. But it does lead us to an important correlation. Should we be concerned about the spiritual direction of an unbaptized 18-year-old? Yes—absolutely.

We return to our earlier concern: why doesn't immersion necessarily mark a major ethical or spiritual redirection in the lives of very young adolescents? If baptism and the decisions leading to it have little immediate impact on a young teen's social life, his family life, his ability to display the fruit of the Spirit, or his belief in God's importance, *how changed is he?* If we reply, "not very much" or "only minimally," does this mean that we have failed to teach biblical conversion properly? Or, worse, does it mean that our children's conversions are half-hearted, even false? Such questions are premature and alarmist, in our view. We suggest at least two external factors, which color the picture considerably, must be considered closely before we offer any judgments about the authenticity of our children's conversions.

First, we must consider the unique nature of "conversions" of persons who come from within—rather than from outside—a religious community. Second, we must consider whether or not we have conveyed an adequate understanding of the conversion process to our children. We first consider the unique circumstance of the conversion of children who come from Christian homes.

U-turn or Signpost?

Our survey of thousands of teens forces us to conclude, overwhelmingly, that most of our teens do choose to be baptized for sound, thoughtful reasons. Yet their conversions appear to be more like those in the Old Testament than those in the Book of Acts. Much of the New Testament's language about conversion describes a missionary setting. It often speaks of the radical transition from paganism to the way of Christ. Peter writes, for example: "You have already spent enough time in doing what the Gentiles like to do, living in licentiousness, passions, drunkenness, revels, carousing, and lawless idolatry" (1 Peter 4:3, NRSV). Paul speaks to Gentile converts in a similar fashion:

> Do you not know that wrongdoers will not inherit the kingdom of God? Do not be deceived! Fornicators, idolaters, adulterers, male prostitutes, sodomites, thieves, the greedy, drunkards, revilers, robbers—none of these will inherit the kingdom of God. (1 Corinthians 6:9-10, NRSV)

Much of the New Testament is concerned with bringing pagan "outsiders" into the Kingdom of God, yet clearly such language does not adequately describe children raised at the feet of godly parents.

By contrast, the Old Testament and some of Jesus' teaching in the Gospels focus more on the repentance of believers, rather than the radical conversion of pagans. God, through his prophets, calls Israel to repudiate idolatry and to return to him, but God does not call the Israelites to convert to Judaism—they were already Jews, people of the covenant. When a Jew decided for himself to follow God, he did not "convert" to a new faith. He reaffirmed the faith which had surrounded him and his family for generations. This kind of conversion might mean changing particular habits of the heart or abandoning particular sins. It did not necessarily call for a total revolution in lifestyle. The adolescents we studied seem to convert in a manner that is more appropriately "Jewish" than "pagan." Most choose to be baptized after having been believers for years. Thus, the changes in belief and behavior are incremental, not radical.

Certainly, this is not a bad pattern. We are glad many children grow up in Christian families, entirely at home in faith communities where the love of God is strong. For these children, baptism is an important signpost on their spiritual journey, but it is seldom the radical U-turn called for in revivalist sermons. As noted in Figure 7.4, fewer than 10% of our teens indicate that baptism significantly changed their social lives. Likewise, only 20% report that baptism changed their family lives. Yet change is reported: over half (60%) report that baptism changed them emotionally, helping them to display the fruit of the Spirit.

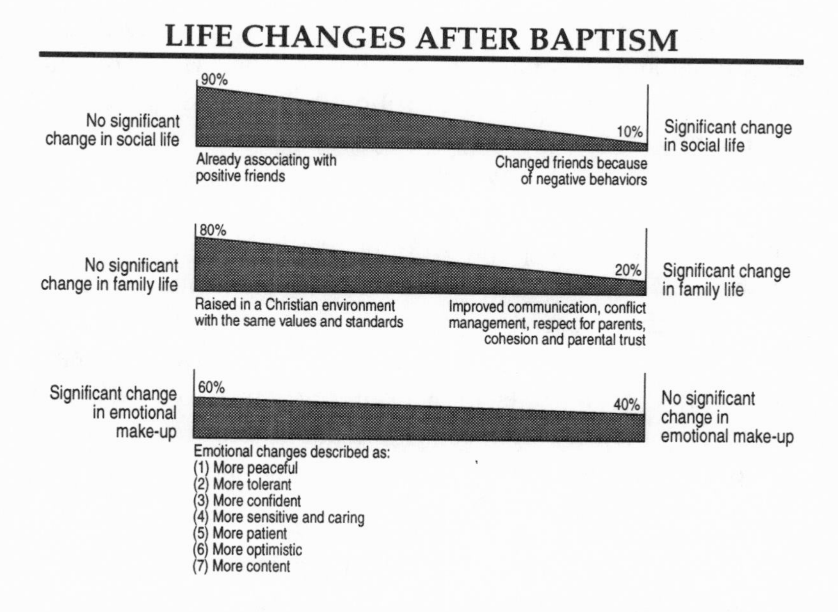

FIGURE 7.4

Enriching the Tradition

The absence of dramatic life changes in our children after baptism may have roots in the community from which they come. It is certainly possible that the ceremony of conversion may have little impact on our teens because it is presented in a way they cannot take too seriously. This will astound some of our readers who think the Churches of Christ, above all Christian groups, have emphasized baptism. Yet it is possible to hold tenaciously to a doctrine even while depleting it of its glory and power. It is possible to promote adult immersion vigorously, yet trivialize it at the same time! We think this has happened in many instances. If one reads the stunning accounts of early Christian baptisms, today's ceremonies, by comparison, appear thin and enervated.

How should our teaching and practice of baptismal rites be different? In general, we must rediscover the emotional and spiritual power of conversion. Baptism, and the events leading up to and following it, must be seen as profoundly significant. Yet today, baptisms are often rather nominal affairs. Many churches baptize people in large assemblies where many of the church-goers, if not most, do not even know the person being baptized. The baptism typically occurs as a hurried addendum to the formal worship, even irritating those who don't want a long service. Shouts of praise, joyful amens, and applause are seldom heard. Tears are limited to parents or a grandparents. In brief, our baptisms—the very signposts of our submission to Christ and his lordship—are often not cherished, celebrated, or intimate. We need something more.

To live godly lives for a lifetime means realizing where we have been, recognizing where we are now, and understanding what may lie ahead. We believe the Christian experience must be at the very least *(1) connected, (2) transformational*, *(3) explicit*, *(4) vivid*, and *(5) community-oriented.* As we attempt to explain these key concepts, it should be understood that they are deeply intertwined. One cannot speak of Christianity being explicit without also demonstrating that it needs to be community-oriented. Each depends on and reinforces the others.

Connected. Baptism, separated from fuller life of the church, has little meaning. We cannot pursue life in a divided fashion, living out events separated from one another: here, our work segment; there, our family segment; next week, our religious segment. All of life must be submitted to God. And baptism must be related to all of life. One of the great problems with baptism is that it has been taught as an isolated doctrine, yet it is utterly meaningless (merely a bath), if it is not continuously linked to a person—Jesus Christ. If baptism does not lead us to consider the life of Jesus, if it does not lead us to think about our call to take up our crosses and imitate him; if it does not stand as a living drama of our willingness to be crucified with him, then the form is meaningless. Baptism is a door, not a destination, a passage into the life of Christ, a means of contact with the living, indwelling Savior.

We must consider other ways in which baptism invites us to connect. Baptism intimately unites us with fellow believers. We are all baptized into one body. Baptism implies unity, fellowship—connectedness. It is a birthing ceremony which introduces us to a vast fellowship of brothers and sisters. It always leads us back to the church, the family of God. Baptism is, of course, by definition an initiation, a commencement. Yet there is a tendency to see it as just the reverse, as the *conclusion* to a process. Baptism ought to be linked to a new role and position in the congregation. There should be plenty of opportunities for new instruction, new growth, new duties, new expectations. Counseling, instruction, and mentoring should follow baptism. Intergenerational experiences should be included so as to connect the new convert to the whole church, not just to a part of it, like the youth group.

Transformational. Until the Roman emperor Constantine's "conversion" in A. D. 311, when Christianity became the official religion of the empire, Christians were in the extreme minority.[1] Before that time, to be a Christian meant sacrifice and persecution.

Life in the Roman Empire was difficult and uncertain. Feelings of uprootedness and alienation were

> pervasive in the population generally, but especially among the marginalized Christians, preeminently the outsiders of society, the objects of suspicion, censure, and hostility.[2]

To become a Christian in the early centuries involved radical change. It meant transformation—becoming a *new form*, different and changed from the past. We hold that the church today falls short of conveying baptism as a truly transforming event, one which ushers one into a new way of being. Dr. Lewis Rambo, Professor of Theology at San Francisco Theological Seminary, agrees that it is imperative to convey to those becoming Christians "that they are separating from the realm of darkness, the powers of evil and that they are now making a transition into the body of Christ in a new and deeper and theologically . . . profound way."[3] Indeed, to choose Christ is to throw off the shackles of Satan and bow before the King of Glory. As our culture slides into an increasingly anti-Christian posture, we should do a much better job of articulating the radical demands that Christ makes on his children. To follow Christ is to take a different path from the world. Baptism should clearly indicate our willingness to be a unique people under the cross.

Explicit. If we are to convey that living for Christ means radical change, we cannot do so subtly or implicitly. We cannot merely say it. We must demonstrate it. To clarify why, let us for a moment consider how young children assign meaning. How do children come to understand that something is special, worthy, or extraordinary? How does a child learn her birthday is a special day? She knows through the gestures of celebration that accompany that day. She receives gifts from friends, she enjoys a tasty cake, and she delights in bright balloons and streamers. Likewise, a child may learn that one of Mommy's dresses is special by the way she treats it. Because this is the only dress which she keeps in a bag, because she wears it only when she also wears glimmering jewelry, and because Mommy always smells especially good when she wears this dress, a child learns that this dress is not merely one among others. Children learn that something is to be regarded or cared for or remembered through explicit gestures and symbols: cake, balloons, jewelry, perfume, and so forth. We do not simply tell a child, "Your birthday is a really special day," and then treat it like any other. Nor do we say, "This dress is Mommy's absolute favorite," and then casually toss it into the laundry basket. We act in explicit and unique ways which are consistent with our statements.

Hence, we ought to promote and celebrate baptism as if it really were the identity-shaping event which we claim it is. If we can cheer on a professional baseball team or celebrate a corporate promotion, certainly a person's public pronouncement of Christ as his Savior is worth celebrating in a big way! Our children can hardly take us seriously if we say mechanically, "This baptism signifies the most important decision you've ever made," and then we act just as we would any other day of the year. If they do not see gestures that proclaim our genuine excitement, they will not believe us. We must celebrate not merely "in word or speech, but in truth and action" (1 John 3:18, NRSV).

A number of activities could help. Parents might have family members, aunts, uncles, cousins, brothers, and sisters, join in a special meal at which the new convert is honored. Friends might write letters of affirmation for the convert. One family we know has the child write a letter to himself about the meaning of his baptism. Later in life, the letter is presented to the child as a reminder of what he knew and felt on that day. (Too many 12-year-olds have made this decision, but have forgotten just how much they did know and understand when they reached 18 or 20.) A new suit of clothes may be entirely in order, as a way of underscoring the biblical point that we are clothed with a new self at baptism. A sunrise baptism, a baptism in a specially meaningful place, or by a special teacher, friend, or mentor—all these details could add meaning to a convert's new beginning.

Vivid. Lewis Rambo also maintains that it is essential for us to celebrate baptism to such a degree that "[n]o matter what is going on in a person's life . . . they will never forget it. No matter how far a person may drift from the body of Christ . . . if they have been baptized into Jesus Christ, there is some hope to draw them back into the fold." As Christians, we must never forget that we have been newly formed into children of God. If we are not to forget, the Christian life must be vivid. By "vivid," we do not mean gilded or melodramatic. We mean that the experiences within the Christian community need to be so clear, pointed, and in contrast to the world, that they indelibly mark us, reminding us we are God's people.

Dr. Patrick Garner of Harding University, drawing on the work of Richard Booker, writes about the vivid context of the ancient Hebraic covenant:

> Implicit in [the steps of covenant] is the notion of mutuality and reciprocity. Parties first remove their coats, take off their belts and weapons, and then cut the covenant. An animal has been killed and split. Both parties walk between the two halves, symbolizing their shedding of personal rights and accepting obligation to the other person through the covenant pact. They then raise their right arms, intermingle blood, exchange names, and rub their cuts to make a scar to remind them of their pact. They also stand before witnesses, state the terms of the covenant, eat a memorial meal, and plant a tree to be a permanent memorial commemorating the relationship. Interestingly, this relationship is binding

> both to the participants, their children and to all their unborn heirs still residing within their bodies.[4]

Undoubtedly, people who participated in this type of covenant ritual, such as David and Jonathan, did not easily forget the meaning or significance of the pact. Such rituals serve not as ends themselves but as means to remember the true end: *respecting and living out the covenant.* The pain of a cut, the sight of blood, and the disfigurement of a scar all impact a person. Both the permanence of a tree and the shared meal also serve to remind the covenant-makers that their covenant is no trifle.

Baptism ought to have an equivalent sort of drama about it. Though there are occasions in the New Testament when baptisms are almost immediate (as in the book of Acts), we know very little about precisely how they were carried out. Baptism seems to have had a lot of prominence in the early churches, according to some of the oldest records from antiquity.[5] For Christians in the second, third, and fourth centuries, baptism was an extremely momentous rite of passage:

> The initiation process dramatizes a cosmic struggle between good and evil . . . The process involved a number of rituals of humiliation—"scrutinies" and "inquiries" (spiritual interrogations), fasting, vigils, and the formal renunciation of Satan, his service and works.[6]

These interrogations served to bring about a time of serious questioning, self-examination, and radical renunciation. Furthermore, the whole ordeal of deciding to submit oneself to Christ and to initiate life through baptism did not occur over a few weeks or even a few months. It lasted *two or three years.* It then concluded in a characteristically vivid manner: "In the Hippolytan rite, [for example,] after an all-night vigil during which the candidates listen to Scripture reading and additional instruction, the elect are stripped, exorcised once more, anointed with oil, and baptized. . . ."[7] To forget his baptism and its transforming meaning, an early Christian would literally have to suffer amnesia. Otherwise, the message of this rite of passage would forever be upon both his heart and lips.

To be sure, we are not advocating some new (or ancient) procedures which involve pain, scrutinies, exorcism, and all-night vigils. But we are reminding our readers that biblical and apostolic rituals were often robust, dramatic, and unforgettable. We believe baptism should powerfully remind converts of their identity in Christ. We believe baptism should echo "the blood covenant cut by Christ, accepted by the believer and renewed constantly by the Eucharist ceremony."[8]

Community-oriented. Throughout this chapter we have asserted the community as essential to the Christian walk. We come to Christ not as isolated individuals, but as connected members of one body. Membership in a community of faith makes us accountable to the lives we have chosen in Christ. The religious community always plays an important role in rites of passage and the formation of covenants. A crucial part of the Hebraic covenant was the stating of the covenant aloud before a group of witnesses. Likewise, early Christian baptisms typically occurred in the midst of a group which encouraged the new convert and held him accountable for his profession. In the case of baptism, as in other events of the Christian life, the community imparts meaning as its members recall the story of Christ and his sacrifice.

By living an explicitly Christ-like life and by using vivid rituals and gestures designed to recall Christ's sacrifice, perhaps we can lead our teens (and ourselves) to act and live with the awareness that we are new people. By expressing meaning through vivid, tangible forms, and through the support of a community of faith, our children can carry the memory of their baptismal promises for a lifetime.

Other Rites of Memory

We do not want to suggest that baptism is the sum of the Christian life. It is not. All of our lives, day in and day out, can be transformational, explicit, vividly lived in community, and connected to Jesus Christ. We believe that various ceremonies in the home, for example, can greatly enhance the spiritual well-being of children. Unfortunately, many forces are encroaching on the sacred space of family and home—television, movies, and an avalanche of after-school activities (sports, music, clubs, etc.). Sadly, there is scarcely any time left for many families to meet and share. It is time to reclaim our homes and make them safe havens for community. Henri Nouwen, the well-known writer on the spiritual life, notes two areas of daily life, meal time and meditations, which can enrich our family life. He speaks first of the community of mealtime:

> Good families always "ritualize" the table. . . . There's *nothing* so important in the family as the sacred quality of the meal. . . . Community means that people come together around the table, not just to feed their bodies, but to feed their minds and their relationships. Good families always ritualize the table. . . . Do you turn off the television? Do you say, "No telephone calls; we're just going to be together, even if for an hour?" That's important. . . . I'm talking about the whole "culture" of the meal. How do we eat? Do we just get it over as soon as possible, or do we say there's a first course which we finish first, then a second course, and so forth? . . . My family ritualized meals. At Christmas we went to church at midnight, and afterwards we had breakfast in the middle of the night.

> And it was always a tradition to invite one or two guests who didn't have a family.
>
> Just a few weeks ago my father invited us all to Holland. . . . [H]e took all of us to a restaurant. During the meal my father welcomed us formally and said, "We're glad you are here. These are some of the things we are grateful for, etc." That is community.[9]

We can also improve our children's spiritual lives (and our own) if we create space for prayer, reflection, and readings. Nouwen adds:

> There are very simple, contemplative rituals. To busy people I suggest a little booklet of daily readings from Scripture. I say to them, "Every morning before you get up read the Gospel of the day. That's all you have to do. Spend two minutes just thinking about it, and say, 'This is the Gospel of the day. I will pray for what I will meet today.'" Now, that's just a three-minute thing. I don't think that's too much to ask.

Nouwen's message is that our faith should completely inform our lives. After all—relationship with Christ *is* life.

Simple rituals within our families and our faith communities can consistently remind us of the one to whom we are dedicated. We encounter believers regularly who have been touched by just this type of family ritual. Beth, a university student, describes how her parents have seized upon this concept, turning an ordinary occasion into a sacred memory:

> For as long as I can remember, my parents have blessed me and my brother on the first day of school each year. I vividly recall the hurry and butterflies of those mornings being interrupted with a few sacred moments.

> Mom would hold our hands or put her arms around us. Dad would firmly lay a hand on each of our heads and say a prayer. He would ask God to nurture us. He would pray for the unknown challenges of that new year. He would rededicate our life as a family to God's glory. Then he would fix us with an intense and loving eye and say, "And now, may the Lord bless you and keep you. May he make his face to shine upon you . . . and bring you peace."
>
> I remember there were years that I dreaded it: It was too awkward to be held that closely to my big brother, or Dad would lay his hand a little *too* firmly on my head, or Mom would start crying. Sometimes it just seemed silly. But even then I knew that it *wasn't* silly. When the blessings came to me each year, I knew that something sacred had broken through.
>
> I guess part of the power of ritual is that its full meaning only comes later—it grows and unfolds over time. Now I know how much it means to have parents who bless me. This year I didn't go home before the fall semester began, so I asked my parents to bless me over the phone. It means too much to me to let a year go by without it.

Beth's story is a beautiful example of how parents can give meaning and purpose to their children through sacred times in the home. As Beth explains, through this family custom, her parents have imparted the unforgettable message of God's importance. They turn an ordinary event—the beginning of school—into a time of sacred significance. We hope more parents will follow this lead. God has provided ample opportunity. Whether it is a holiday or a family reunion, a birthday or a marriage, a homecoming or a separation occasioned by a business trip or a journey to summer camp, we can foster family traditions which consistently remind each member, "You are important. God is with you. You have a destiny to glorify God." Such activities help break down the walls which compartmentalize our lives. They reunite us to one another and to our lives in Christ.

Bright Chains of Loving Rite

George Rawson is the poet who wrote the great words to A. H. Troyte's Chant "By Christ Redeemed, In Christ Restored." In that hymn, Rawson envisioned the Lord's Supper as "one bright chain of loving rite" that spiritually links all Christians living between Gethsemane and the Second Coming of Christ:

> And thus that dark betrayal night
> With the last advent we unite,
> By one bright chain of loving rite,
> Until he come.

We would add that uniting all the believers between Gethsemane and the Second Coming is the function of all Christian ceremonies; but baptism preeminently links us to the passion of Jesus, his suffering on the cross, and his promised return. It also links us to the fellowship of saints who await his appearing. It unites us to the one body, and it quickens our dull, faulty memories. We live in a fragmented and chaotic culture. Our children are, like their parents, sadly forgetful. Luis Buñuel writes, "Memory is what makes our lives. Life without memory is no life at all. . . . Our memory is our coherence, our reason, our feeling, even our action. Without it, we are nothing. . . ."[10] While Buñuel is thinking in secular terms, his thoughts apply well to the life of believers. We are in desperate trouble if we cannot remember. God has given us "loving rites" to help us. Our children especially need them.

We thank God that the teens we surveyed approach baptism in seriousness. Our hope is that all of us, through a renewed appreciation of baptism and other rites of memory, will see that the whole of life—social, family, congregational, and all—is no longer the domain of Satan, but the sacred territory of God.

---

[1] John Howard Yoder, *The Priestly Kingdom: Social Ethics as Gospel* (Notre Dame: Notre Dame UP, 1984) 135.

[2] Darryl Tippens, "Reading at Cockcrow: Oral Reception and Ritual Experience in Mark's Passion Narrative," *Essays in Literature* 20.1 (Spring 1993): 150.

[3] Lewis Rambo, "The Many Faces of Christ": Abilene Christian University's Youth and Family Conference, Feb. 1992.

[4] Patrick Garner, "New Testament Words Associated with Communication and Spirituality," Speech Communication Association, Miami, Nov. 1993.

[5] Tippens, "Reading at Cockcrow," 149-50. See also Thomas Finn, "It Happened One Saturday Night: Ritual and Conversion in Augustine's North Africa," *Journal of the American Academy of Religion* 58 (1990): 589-616; and Finn, "Ritual Process and the Survival of Early Christianity: A Study in the Apostolic Tradition of Hippolytus," *Ritual Studies* 3 (1989): 69-84.

[6] Tippens, "Reading at Cockcrow," 150.

[7] Tippens, "Reading at Cockcrow," 151.

[8] Garner.

[9] "Loneliness and Community: An Interview with Henri Nouwen." *Wineskins* 2.7 (1994): 15-16.

[10] Qtd. in Oliver Sacks, *The Man Who Mistook His Wife for a Hat and Other Clinical Tales* (New York: Summit Books, 1985).

8

Congregational Life and Faith Formation

So then, brothers and sisters, stand firm and hold fast to the traditions that you were taught by us, either by word of mouth or by our letter. —2 Thessalonians 2:15

Because Christian community is founded solely on Jesus Christ, it is a spiritual and not a [human] reality. —Dietrich Bonhoeffer

[X-ers] see [boomers] as insufferably self-righteous yuppies who sold out their principles, placed work over family and money making over community. —Joseph Shapiro

Students and commencement speakers frequently say, as graduates leave their institutions of learning, that they are going out into the "real world." This is a fascinating expression, since it implies that school life is not "real." Presumably, the real is somewhere out there beyond the campus boundaries, beyond books, lectures, final exams, and football games. The real must be about payroll taxes, home mortgages, work schedules, and retirement funds. A similar division between the "real world" and the "unreal" seems to creep into many people's thinking about church. Church is good. Church is fine. But in a patronizing way, some people talk as though what goes on in church is very different from the "real world" of hard-nosed business deals and corporate ladders. In this way, church is reduced to a kind of "cosmic relief" from the heat of real, raw competition. In other words, church is some place outside the arena of the real world.

We reject this unbiblical (and simple-minded) division between the "real world" and the "unreal." If by "real" we mean "true" or "valid," then wherever one approaches God and his truth, one is coming into the presence of the Real. If the church is the place where grace and truth are taught, honored, and lived, then when one enters into worship with the faith community, one is inhabiting the "real world." In the ancient church, nonbelievers would sometimes visit a Christian assembly. What happened there was so remarkable, so life-affirming, worshipful and awe-inspiring that these nonbelievers would bow down before God and exclaim, "God is really among you" (1 Corinthians 14:25, NIV). In doing so, they were saying, "We have found the Real!" To worship in spirit is to worship in truth, to enter into the real (John 4:24).

By the same token, any place that does not recognize, admit, or honor God is a false domain. This is a constant theme in C. S. Lewis's writings. The ordinary workaday world was for Lewis the "shadowlands"—the false, the insubstantial. We enter the real world as we move towards God and his heavenly reality. With Lewis, we challenge the idolatry of our age that recognizes only the concrete and the material as real.

Finding Our Souls in Church

Meeting God in worship is the truest experience known to human beings. One of the finest examples of this truth is borne out in a remarkable case reported by Dr. Oliver Sacks, a distinguished neurologist and the author of *Awakenings* and other books about people with neurological problems. One of Sacks's patients was Jimmy, a handsome, healthy 49-year-old man who seemed normal in every way, except he was experiencing a terrible form of amnesia. Jimmy had a full and interesting life. He remembered his early life vividly. He could recall his life as a sailor in the U.S. Navy, the end of World War II, and his thoughts of the future. But his memory stopped abruptly and absolutely with the year 1945. Anything that happened after that date was forgotten, literally within a few seconds. There were gaping holes in his life story, for he had lost decades of his life in a huge black hole of amnesia. He was a victim of what is called Korsakov's Syndrome, an illness that causes permanent memory loss. The man's life was devastated. Sacks described him as a "lost soul," a spiritual casualty. Yet something very strange happened when this man went to church.

One day Sacks observed Jimmy during a communion service in a chapel. During the service, as Jimmy partook of the Lord's Supper, the physician saw a remarkable change:

> I was moved, profoundly moved and impressed, because I saw here an intensity and steadiness of attention and concentration that I had never seen before in him or conceived him capable of. . . . Fully, intensely, quietly, in the quietude of absolute concentration and attention, he entered and partook of Holy Communion. He was wholly held, absorbed, by a feeling. There was no forgetting, no Korsakov's

> then, nor did it seem possible or imaginable that there should be. . . . Clearly Jimmy found himself, found continuity and reality, in the absoluteness of spiritual attention and act. . . . He did find his soul here. . . . Seeing Jim in the chapel opened my eyes to other realms where the soul is called on, and held, and stilled, in attention and communion.[1]

Sacks observed that something powerful and mysterious happened to Jimmy in worship. Jimmy did not escape "the real" when he attended worship. Quite the reverse; he was encountering it. We find a spiritual message in Jimmy's story. When we find God, we find the Real, and we find our own souls. In the presence of God we become more completely whole, healthy and sane. In Pauline terms the experience of the Gospel is healthy or "hygienic" (Titus 2:2). We wonder: does congregational life, the place where the Gospel is allegedly proclaimed and enacted, encourage healthy living and a spiritual outlook? Does spiritual formation take place in our congregations?

The purpose of this chapter is two-fold. First, we report our teens' replies to a number of fundamental issues. How do our teens view their home churches? How does the church contribute to their spiritual formation? What happens to our teens when they go to church? What encourages them to take God seriously in their lives? There is much to report on these topics.

Our second objective is to describe the kind of communities we believe we must build if we are to be faithful both to Scripture and to our young. We are convinced that our children will face several major spiritual crises before they reach maturity. Churches with a business-as-usual mindset will be poorly equipped to protect their children against the powerful attractions of an aggressively secular society. Parents and church leaders must take their God-given mission earnestly and militantly if they intend to transmit the Christian faith to the next generation. Above all, they must reconsider what it means to be a community of faith in our day and time. They will honestly concede that many vibrant churches in previous centuries failed to transmit the Gospel to their children. Extinction resulted.

Today's churches which care about their children will rediscover elements of body life that are taught in Scripture which have been obscured by our cultural biases. We will rediscover the value of Christian memory and tradition, storytelling and testimony, a sense of the sacred, spiritual mentoring, and blessing our children. We begin first with the data.

Ministry and Church System

What happens when the church comes together is a paramount issue for teens. We asked the teens in our study to evaluate various elements of congregational life: youth ministry, preaching, Bible classes, and elders. We then compared two groups: the teens who positively valued each of these church ministries and those who negatively valued them. We consistently found that the teens who view a particular ministry positively take God much more seriously than those that do not. For instance, as Figure 8.1 illustrates, 41% of teens who appreciate youth ministry take God seriously compared to only 29% of those who do not value youth ministry.

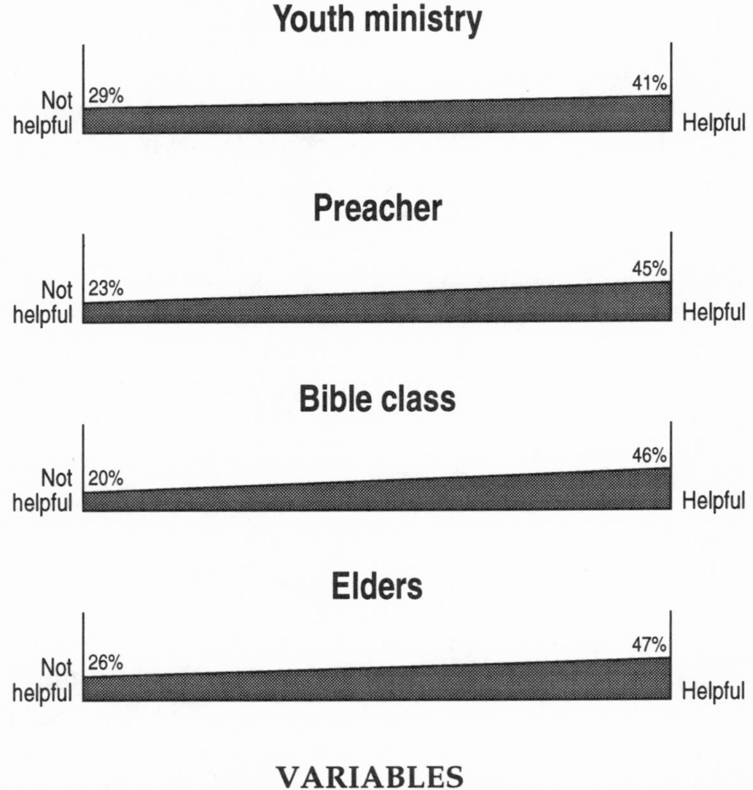

FIGURE 8.1

Our study also examined the adolescents' home churches. The teens placed their churches along each of five continuums:

- Legalistic vs. grace-oriented
- Grudge-holding vs. forgiving
- Out of touch vs. relevant
- Insensitive vs. sensitive
- Unsupportive vs. supportive

This evaluation was then statistically correlated with various measures of spiritual attitudes. Teens who view their congregations positively (that is, as grace-oriented, forgiving, relevant, sensitive, and supportive) are much more likely to view God as helpful than are teens from churches which they perceive as legalistic, grudge-holding, and insensitive. For example, 75% of the teens from grace-oriented churches indicated significant spiritual maturity compared with only 58% of the teens from legalistic churches. Additionally, adolescents from positive churches exhibited more ethical, moral, and Christ-centered decision-making than did teens from negative churches. The character or personality of a congregation does affect the spirituality and the attitudes of teenagers.

Our research did reveal one exception in the pattern of positive churches aiding in spiritual formation. Congregations which do not project a consistent personality or point of view are problematic. As shown in Figure 8.2, teens who come from churches that are neither legalistic nor grace-oriented consider God less important than teens from churches which are either legalistic or grace-oriented. In other words, teens from *identity-confused* congregations are the least likely to take God seriously.

The psychologist Erik Erikson asserts that the primary purpose of adolescence is to establish one's identity—that is, to come to know what one is about. He warns that a person who never achieves this purpose will remain emotionally stunted, even in adulthood. If we expect teens to learn who they truly are—the beloved children of the Most High God—church leaders must be people who know who they are. We cannot expect our adolescents to blossom into spiritual giants if our churches do not contain adult models who embody spiritual maturity.

IMPORTANCE OF GOD AND CHURCH SYSTEM

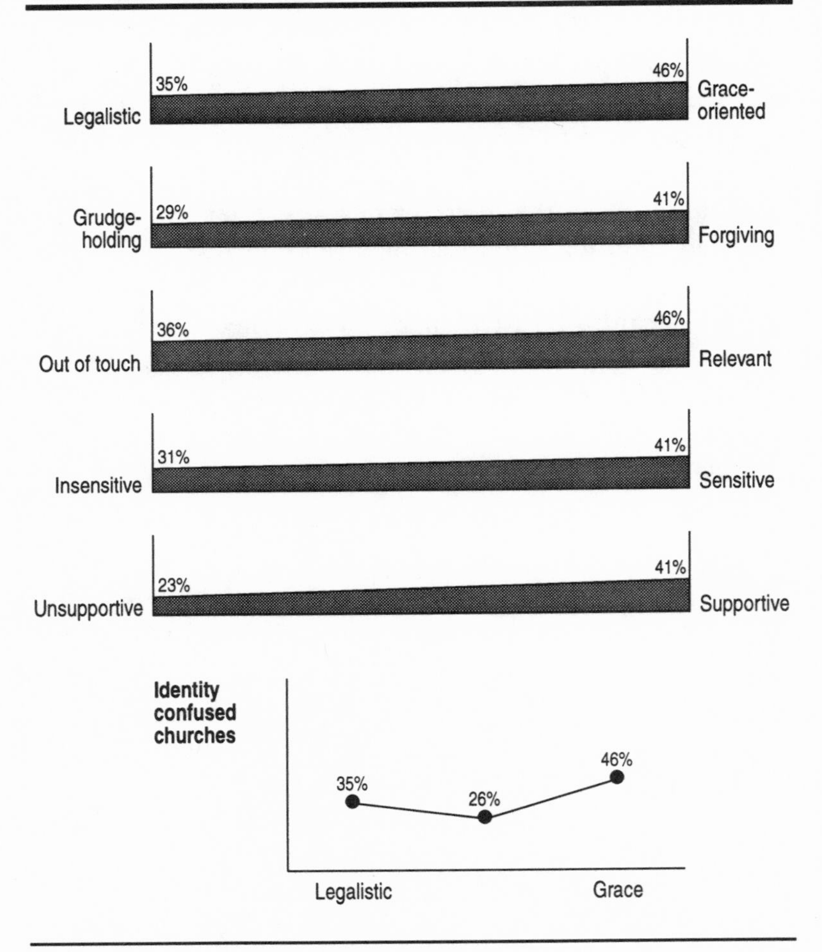

FIGURE 8.2

The ability to help teens take God seriously will surely affect whether they stay in the church. We asked the teens to evaluate how many of them remain in the church after graduating from high school. The data shown in Figure 8.3 confirms our suspicions that about one-half of teens leave the Churches of Christ after graduation from high school. Furthermore, it appears that about one-third totally lose faith in Christ.

YOUTH ATTRITION

Youth group's present involvement in church

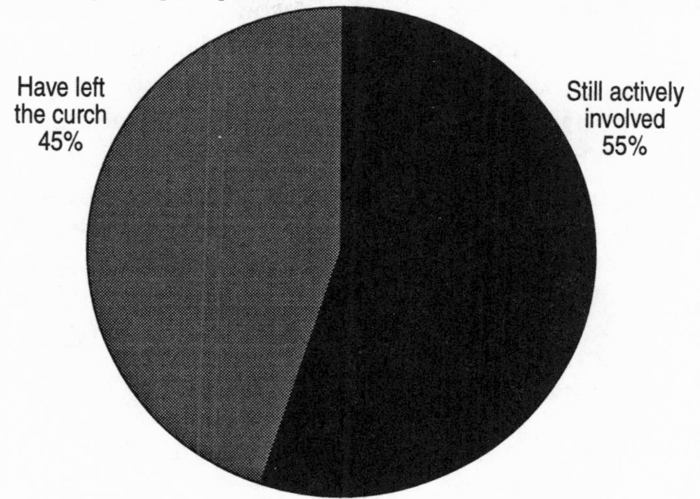

Youth group's present faith in Christ

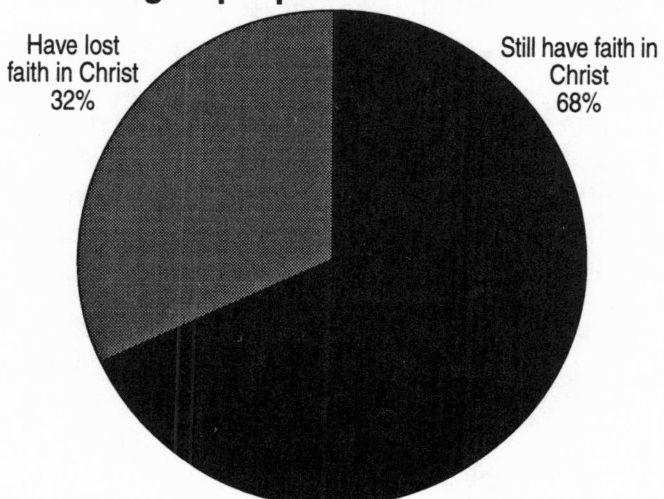

- Data represent responses of high school graduates only.

FIGURE 8.3

In view of the long-established trend that many of our young abandon the faith—or, at least, the religious affiliation of their fathers and mothers—it is imperative that we evaluate and rediscover the spiritual mission and meaning of the church. As we consider the history of Christianity and the fact that the faith is in decline in areas of the world where it once burned brightly, we must ask the same question Jesus asked: "When the Son of Man comes, will he find faith on earth?" (Luke 18:8, NIV). What can we do to sponsor spiritual renewal, to ensure faithful communities of Christians for our children and our children's children? We offer five suggestions.

Communities That Believe

First, we need communities that believe in community. Ironically, too many Christians have lost their sense of relatedness. An excessive allegiance to individualism has radically distorted our thinking, as Robert Bellah and others have pointed out. We have become isolated souls floating in space, hermetically sealed off from others.[2] Yet God designed us to live in community. We are conceived in community, born, reared, and saved in community, and we shall die in community. Heaven is the joyous consummation of community—an eternal wedding banquet—and hell is the absolute loss of community.

Our power to resist evil, our capacity to love, our sense of mission, and our very identities are shaped by community. Scriptural ethics presupposes that we neither enter nor escape the messes of our lives purely by our own volition. We get into trouble through the persuasive agency of others; and we are saved by the persuasive intervention of others. The modern notion of the "self-formed" identity is inaccurate and heretical. We do not achieve our identities in a vacuum; our identities are shaped by other selves, communities, and histories. We are "one body, members one of another" (Romans 12:5, NRSV).

If we really had a biblical view of the self—that is, if we critiqued the American myth of the self—we would do church differently. We would come to see how grace, love, and mercy are not only gifts from God, sent from on high. They are also gifts from God *transmitted through one another*. Healing and holiness come through the very ones who walk and work beside us. Since faith is always born in community, we must become profoundly dissatisfied with any congregational life that is superficial or merely social. We will build fellowships where we know one another and where we are accountable to each other.

Remembering the Past

Second, for communities to be healthy, they must renew their appreciation for their past. Memory is critical to survival. Indeed, no community is possible without a sense of the past, and no past could ever exist without a community to preserve it, revere it, and transmit it. Religious communities *especially* rely on and value the past. In *Fiddler on the Roof,* Tevye sings "Tradition!", for in his heart he knows that with the death of tradition comes the death of community, followed soon by the death of the self.

Cultural radicals object to a focus on the past, not just because the tradition may be "sexist," "racist," or "imperialist," but because they understand that the stories from the past shape our identities and keep us faithful to traditional values. Our past stories tell us that we are created in God's image and destined to serve him. This past is being silently deleted from our classrooms in order to "liberate" us from our God-connectedness. Without these stories we are free to be anything at all—or, more truly, nothing at all.

In the nineteenth century Alexis de Toqueville studied the American democratic experiment, and he prophesied with uncanny accuracy that democracy might breed a spirit of excessive self-sufficiency. People who grow up in a democracy easily think that they owe no one anything; they think for themselves, imagining that

> their whole destiny is in their own hands. Thus, not only does democracy make men forget their ancestors, but it also clouds their view of their descendants and isolates them from their contemporaries. Each man is forever thrown back on himself alone, and there is danger that he may be shut in the solitude of his own heart.[3]

Many American Christians today—cut off from their past—are exactly in this position. In such an historical vacuum it is exceedingly hard to develop spirituality.

Who are we? Believers used to recite repeatedly the story of their past. They said something like this: "My father was a homeless Aramean who went down to Egypt and lived there with a small band of people, but there he became a great, powerful, and large nation" (Deuteronomy 26:5, NRSV). In the stories of Scripture and in the legends of the exemplary lives of the people of God, believers found their own personal identities. Unfortunately, American values and the codes of modernity have tempted us to forget our past, both secular and spiritual. We have preferred Henry Ford ("History is more or less bunk") over God ("Remember the former things of old, for I am God, and there is no other" Isaiah 46:9, NRSV).

Faithful communities will rediscover and reconstruct tradition. Tradition is not a dirty word. It is the very element of culture, the mode of thought and behavior passed from one generation to another, the sum of how we do things. No family can survive without a sense of shared ways of doing things, and neither can a church family. Paul says:

> So then, my brothers and sisters, stand firm and hold fast to the traditions that you were taught by us, either by word of mouth or by letter . . . Keep away from believers who are . . . not [living] according to the tradition that they received from us. (2 Thessalonians 2:15, 3:6, NRSV)

Respecting the Sacred

Third, we must restore a sense of the holy. Albert Camus once wrote that our era is defined by a rebellious spirit, particularly in the area of religion and values:

> The present interest in the problem of rebellion only springs from the fact that nowadays whole societies have wanted to discard the sacred. We live in an unsacrosanct moment in history.[4]

Our culture is attempting to abolish the category of the sacred. In his recent articles and books, Michael Medved demonstrates persuasively how the media subjects the sacred to ridicule.[5] Ironically, both secular society and the church cooperate in this deadly maneuver. Unfortunately, even some churches have so modernized their concept of church and worship that they have diminished the sense of the holy. It is possible to grow up in a church having little experience of awe, transcendence, or sanctity. How many of our children are introduced to the mysterious, unapproachable, holy, jealous, incomparable God who is a consuming fire (Hebrews 12:28-29)? Despite the secular direction of society and our churches, our children remain spiritual creatures who need to worship a mysterious and powerful deity, one who exacts awe and reverence. Robert Coles' *The Spiritual Life of Children* illustrates how children are naturally religious and spiritual. However, they will turn to the false (the occult, New Age) if we do not lead them to the true. We must make space for the holy, and we must rediscover it ourselves.

Restoring Mentors to Our Young

Fourth, we must again hold up proper mentors and heroes. If anything is obvious in our culture, it is that we are woefully short on heroes. Dennis DeYoung of the rock group Styx summarizes the feelings of many Generation X-ers when he confesses, "[E]very day I'm more confused as the saints turn into sinners." He adds, "And I feel this empty place inside—so afraid I've lost my faith." The time has come to call for a new hero—one who challenges the idols of the tribe and the marketplace, yet one who shows the strength of humility and who believes in relationships, stability, and character; who protects and defends; who believes in the holy and reveres it. If Jesus were living today, how would he be incarnated? To answer that question is to name the kind of mentor we need today.

Our goal as teachers, leaders, and ministers is to present to our youth the models and the traditions that will give them a Christian identity. In effect we must give them the materials from which they can construct some true notion of God. Great spiritual biographies and autobiographies like Dietrich Bonhoeffer's *Letters and Papers from Prison*, Augustine's *Confessions* and Henri Nouwen's *The Road to Daybreak* are able to do this.

One of our greatest needs is for compassionate men and women to make themselves available to our children in many ways. We need congregations, in other words, where our children have many parents, brothers, and sisters. In such a setting our children will not lack mentors or models. Jesus asks, "Who is my mother, and who are my brothers?" He points to the disciples—in other words, the church—and says,

"Here are my mother and my brothers" (Matthew 12:49, NIV). If we had churches with many adults functioning as caring surrogate parents to all our children, we would offer our children alternatives, collective wisdom and patterns for living. And we would thus counter the alienation sweeping over our youth. If the church really were the church, our children would be led naturally into an adult life of faith.

The Blessing

Finally, we must bless our children. Dr. William Willimon, the distinguished chaplain at Duke University, has noted a disturbing trend among the youth who are coming to our colleges today. In many cases, they are coming from homes in which parents are either physically or emotionally absent. Parents have been so preoccupied with their careers and personal interests that they have more or less abandoned their children. The college students Willimon sees on campus are lost and lonely, he says. Dr. James Farabino describes a new class of self-centered parents: "Decisions aren't made on the basis of what's best for the child, but what can the child tolerate. With infants, it is how soon can they go to day care so the parents can go to work. With eight- and nine-year-olds, it's how soon can they come home alone."[6] This is just one way in which our culture seems to have forgotten how to bless its children. For children to survive, for children to succeed, we must be present, and we must bless them. We must say good words *to* them. We must say good words *over* them. And we must say good words *about* them. Without affirmation, it is almost impossible to make it in this world. Each and every child deserves to hear: "You are my beloved son or daughter. I thank God for you. I cherish you. You are God's remarkable creation. I will always, always love you."

In James Joyce's novel *Portrait of the Artist as a Young Man*, the young hero Stephen Dedalus tries to explain to his best friend why he must leave Ireland in order to realize his dreams as a writer: "Do you know what Ireland is? asked Stephen with cold violence. Ireland is the old sow that eats her farrow." Stephen's view of his homeland is a fair description of secular America's spiritual treatment of her young. In the name of free speech and free enterprise, "respectable" corporations are free to pour any kind of poison into our children's minds and hearts. As we look at a country in which schools are founded on models of competition that chew up the weak; as we view homes where ambitious parents expend their children for some adult's "professional" advancement; as we think of universities where professors are rewarded for *not* mentoring students, we can only conclude that our society is collectively devouring our progeny, our futures, ourselves.

In apostate Israel, people literally sacrificed their children to the idol Molech. They set up loathsome idols in the temple and then butchered and burned their sons and daughters to honor Molech. The Lord was horrified at this holocaust. God exclaims, "I never commanded [it], nor did it come into my mind" (Jeremiah 7:31, NRSV). It challenges our belief that any culture would sacrifice its children for anything as mundane as power, money, or self-gratification. But ours is doing it.

The Christian community was created to offer a different path, one that blesses the children. The Africans have a saying, "It takes a whole village to raise a child." That's the point. Our sons and daughters need many mothers and fathers. And that is one of the purposes of the church. We bless by loving, confirming, and affirming our children. We bless by admiring our young and speaking well of them. In a very striking section of his popular PBS program *A Gathering of Men,* Robert Bly claims that if a young man does not have a mentor who is constantly admiring him in his youth, then a huge chasm opens in his soul that fills with "demons." We have met many of these young men who wrestle with demons of self-doubt, anger, and spiritual confusion because they did not have a mentor at crucial stages of life.

What do our children need? They need someone who accepts them unconditionally—someone who makes them feel valuable and who confers significance by blessing them. How do we do this? *We look at them closely.* There is plenty of evidence that many children today are not carefully noticed by their parents (or anyone else). Though they live under the same roof, they live mostly separate lives, sealed up in a youth culture defined by their own music, modes of dress, thought patterns and symbols—and the parents are limited by a different adult culture. We will be limited in our ability to help our children until we share with them, once again, a common culture.

We also bless them when we elevate compassion above judgment. Anthony de Mello tells this parable in his book *The Song of the Bird:*

> I was a neurotic for years. I was anxious and depressed and selfish. Everyone kept telling me to change. I resented them, and I agreed with them, and I wanted to change, but simply couldn't, no matter how hard I tried. What hurts the most was that, like the others, my best friend kept insisting that I change. So I felt powerless and trapped.
>
> Then one day, he said to me, "Don't change. Don't change. Don't change . . . I love you as you are." I relaxed. I came alive. And suddenly I changed! Now I know that I couldn't really change, until I found someone who would love me whether I changed or not. Isn't this how God loves us?[7]

We need to convince our children of our all-embracing, unconditional love for them. Such love will bring redemption to them.

We also bless our children when we balance competition with nurture. Henri Nouwen marvels at the competitiveness of society: "The astonishing thing is that the battle for survival has become so 'normal' that few people really believe that it can be different."[8] Our young are desperate for space where they can find approval, freedom, and acceptance without performance.

We bless our children when we model the downward mobility of Jesus. We must radically challenge the "upward mobility" of society that says life is about wealth, status, and power. Instead, in Nouwen's terms, we should adopt the descending way of Jesus. "Downward mobility" means restoring the spirit of the beatitudes to our lives.

Finally, we bless our children when we choose love over power. Malcolm Muggeridge used to tell a story about a soldier wandering in the Western desert who discovers an ancient stone with this inscription: "There are only two possible pursuits, love and power, and no man can have both." Most people choose the way of power. Jesus was offered—and declined—this route in the Wilderness Temptations. If we love our children in the name of Jesus, we must choose love over power. If we do not, we may end up—even in the name of religion!— offering our children to the fashionable deities of our day. And our children will cry out to God as living reminders of all that we failed to do.

In some ways our children are like Jimmy, the tragic amnesiac who wandered into Dr. Sacks' office. Jimmy was a man who had lost his memory, his past, and therefore himself. But in church, "Jimmy found himself, found continuity and reality, in the absoluteness of spiritual attention and action." Best of all, he found his soul. We believe the true church of God functions like this for all the people. But for it to happen, we must be sure that the church is functioning as the true community of God and that we, its adult members, are serving as spiritual fathers and mothers to all our children.

---

[1] Oliver Sacks, *The Man Who Mistook His Wife for a Hat and Other Clinical Tales* (New York: Summit Books, 1985) 36.

[2] Robert Bellah, *Habits of the Heart: Individualism and Commitment in American Life* (New York: Harper and Row, 1986).

[3] Qtd. in Sheena Gillespie, *Literature Across Cultures* (Needham Heights, MA: Allyn and Bacon, 1994) 289.

[4] Qtd. in Richard Abcarian and Marvin Klotz, eds., *Literature: The Human Experience* 4th ed. (New York: St. Martin's, 1968) 722.

[5] Michael Medved, *Hollywood vs. America: Popular Culture and the War on Traditional Values* (New York: HarperCollins, 1992). See also "Popular Culture and the War Against Standards," *Imprimis* Feb. 1991: 1-7. See also Stephen L. Carter, *The Culture of Disbelief: How American Law and Politics Trivialize Religious Devotion* (New York: Basic Books, 1993).

[6] Qtd. in Jerry Adler, "Kids Growing Up Scared," *Newsweek* 10 Jan. 1994: 47-48.

[7] Anthony de Mello, *The Song of the Bird* (New York: Image, 1981) 67-68.

[8] Henri Nouwen, *The Road to Daybreak: A Spiritual Journey* 2nd ed. (New York: Image, 1990) 184.

9

The Imitation of Christ in Our Time

The ultimate purpose of God is to make Christs of us.
—Frederick Buechner

Therefore be imitators of God. —Ephesians 5:2

God is comprehended not by investigation but by imitation.
—Hugh of St. Cher

Saul Bellow, the American novelist, tells the story of visiting Israel where he spent some time at a kibbutz near Caesarea. It was an unusual place, because just below the surface lay a virtually forgotten Roman city dating from ancient times. One day while farming, some locals turned up an entire Roman street. One evening, Bellow explains, he attended a garden party in which everyone sat on the capitals of old Roman columns. Fragments of a forgotten era were evident everywhere in the settlement. Today's Christians are like those Israeli farmers when it comes to the foundations of our spirituality. We live atop an enormous religious tradition that could teach us how to transmit faith to the next generation, yet we have settled for a pottery fragment here and a piece of an old column there.

We have either ignored or forgotten a great deal that could enrich the faith of our children. In this chapter we hope to refresh our memories, to help us remember ancient ways of forming faith that have been largely lost to us.

Perhaps an introductory note is in order here. Throughout this book, we have reported extensive empirical evidence concerning the thoughts, beliefs, and behaviors of our teens. Perhaps for some of our readers, we have provided more charts, graphs, and numbers than they cared to see. We have done this, however, because we find this factual, quantitative data unique and invaluable as we try to make intelligent decisions about how to minister to teens. But now, for awhile, we want to stop analyzing and begin reflecting on the ministry implications of all these numbers. This chapter will be a little different from the preceding ones. We want to lay aside the charts and graphs in order to think about a central biblical theme which we believe is the answer to many of the problems listed in the earlier chapters. We believe the empirical numbers presented in the first eight chapters ultimately call us to return to Scripture so that we might rediscover the biblical meaning of discipleship. That is what this chapter is about.

We believe the best—and most biblical—way to develop spiritual children is through a process the Bible calls "imitation." God calls all people to reflect the divine life of Jesus Christ. This notion is much more ancient than Thomas à Kempis' fifteenth-century treatise, *The Imitation of Christ.* In fact, imitation is rooted in the Old Testament call to replicate the moral life of God: "Be holy for I am holy" says God. Over and over in Scripture, the concept of *imitatio Christi,* "the imitation of Christ," is expressed.[1] We are urged to "Be good imitators" (1 Peter 3:18, NRSV), to have the "same mind that was in Christ Jesus" (Philippians 2:5, NRSV), and to die to self so that Christ can dwell in us (Galatians 2:19-20). The essential point about "putting on Christ" in baptism is a simple, but surprising truth: *Christians are supposed to look like Jesus.* That is the whole point of discipleship: "A disciple is not above the teacher, but everyone who is fully qualified will be like the teacher" (Luke 6:40, NRSV).

Of course, our reflection of Jesus' life is imperfect. Disciples never mirror Jesus as perfectly as they ought; nonetheless, the imitation of Christ remains the central goal of the Christian life. C. S. Lewis says that the "sacrifice of Christ is repeated, or re-echoed, among His followers in varying degrees," through the power of God working in our lives. God guides us in the process as we haltingly "copy" Christ's story into the story of our own lives: "The terrible task [of dying to self] has already been done for us. . . . [T]he master's hand is holding ours as we attempt to trace the difficult letters and . . . our script need only be a 'copy,' not an original. . . ."[2] Here, Lewis is building on Paul's fundamental notion that the life of ordinary Christians can somehow reflect the divine life of Jesus. True spirituality is not a matter of memorizing lots of Scripture texts; nor is it performing miraculous feats—but it is acting, thinking, and looking like Jesus, of "being transformed into the same image from one degree of glory to another" (2 Corinthians 3:18, NRSV). Though we are "clay jars"—afflicted, struck down, and forsaken—we are still imitations of the Lord, "carrying in the body the death of Jesus, so that the life of Jesus may also be made visible in our bodies" (2 Corinthians 4:7-10, NRSV).

Receiving Imitation as a Gift

How does this transformation into the character of Jesus occur? *First, we receive it as a gift from God.* The New Testament asserts over and over that transformation is the work of God. He changes us. He predestined us to be conformed to the image of Jesus Christ (Romans 8:29). We are the recipients of God's miraculous craftsmanship. Our "image" is the work of the Spirit of Jesus (2 Corinthians 3:18). In Eugene Peterson's unforgettable paraphrase, it is "God's gift from start to finish! We don't play the major role. . . . No, we neither make nor save ourselves. God does both the making and the saving" (Ephesians 2:8-9, *The Message*). Sometimes, people who emphasize the spiritual disciplines appear to push a kind of salvation by works, but such is not at all necessary or proper. Spirituality is not the product of human achievement.[3] But we don't just wait passively. We have a role in our transformation.

Meditating on the Model

Second, imitation grows out of envisioning the life and work of Jesus. Historically, Christians used to spend much of their spiritual energies reflecting deeply on the life of Jesus, not just to know the facts, but to appropriate them. One "builds" the cross of Christ by ruminating on the Passion, Christians used to believe. This understanding survives in hymns like "O Sacred Head," "Were You There When They Crucified My Lord?", and "When I Survey the Wondrous Cross."

As hearts and minds dwell upon Jesus and his sufferings, believers find themselves slowly being shaped into his image. We need to rediscover how to experience the story of Jesus so that it can be personally appropriated to our lives and to our children's lives; for how can we "follow in his steps" if we do not have those steps deeply imprinted on our hearts? And how can we have those steps deeply imprinted on our hearts unless we make the life of Jesus a constant meditation?

Before Luther's age, believers heard the New Testament events in a special way: as "paradigmatic acts and gestures," that is, as exemplary stories and patterns that were to be appropriated, replicated, and *enacted* in believers' lives, according to Otto Gründler. Johann Staupitz, a contemporary to Luther, explained the spiritual effects of dwelling upon the life of Jesus:

> On a hill of Calvary he has shown us a model of all sanctity. . . . He is a model given by God, according to which I would work, suffer and die. He is the only model which one can follow, in which every good in life, suffering and death is usefully modeled. Therefore, no one can do right, suffer correctly, or die rightly, unless it happens in conformity with the life, suffering and death of Christ.[4]

After Luther, however, biblical texts were often treated more cerebrally and impersonally. Faithfulness came to mean the acceptance of conceptual meanings which were to be trusted, rather than enacted. In other words, as Otto Gründler explains, *explication* replaced *meditation*, and external promise replaced interior experience.

This discussion of how we approach the text may seem removed from questions about our children's faith development, but in fact the issue is crucial. With the desperate spiritual needs of our children in full view, we must ask: Which is the more biblical method of reading the Bible? If the Bible text does not become our personal story, where is its power?[5] If we would save our children, we will not only lead them back to the Bible, but we will lead them to read the Bible personally and meditatively (as well as analytically). The Bible must be more than a "Guinness Book of Sacred Facts."

Hearing the Word

Imitating Christ in the early church seems to have grown out of a particular oral approach to the Bible. Whereas we talk about *studying* the Bible in an academic an intellectual way, the first disciples sought ways to hear it, receive it, and absorb it. Indeed, Bible study as we practice it today is a modern concept that arose with the invention of the printing press in the fifteenth century, followed by the availability of inexpensive books and universal education. For thousands of years prior to the printing press, God's people most commonly passed on spiritual truths orally and communally. Of course, there was always a small group of literate believers, the scribes, who maintained and preserved manuscript texts. But most of the early Christians were illiterate. Had they been literate, we might add, they would have had little to read, since hand-copied books were expensive and rare.

The point must be emphasized: before the Gutenberg revolution, spiritual formation was, *out of necessity,* communal and oral. Though the Bible was always at the center of spiritual formation, the Bible was used in these oral settings in ways very different from our contemporary "scholastic" models. We are mistaken if we suppose the reading strategies we use today (deriving from modern print culture) were employed in the ancient Christian community.[6]

The early church experienced the Bible in lively communities where the Scriptures were read aloud publicly. Ancient texts, including the Bible, were nearly always read out loud, even if the reading was being done alone. Hundreds of verses refer to *hearing* the word but few talk about *reading* it. The few texts that do refer to "reading" usually speak of reading aloud to an assembly: "Blessed is he who reads aloud the word of prophecy, and blessed are those who hear" (Revelation 1:3, NRSV). This custom of public, oral reading was the universal custom of the ancient world, at least into the fifth century. Augustine, in the *Confessions*, records his profound surprise when he encounters Ambrose, the Bishop of Milan, reading silently in the fifth century.[7]

We are not, of course, trying to turn back the clock in order to pretend that we live in a first-century culture. On the other hand, we must remind ourselves that spiritual growth and maturity do not necessarily depend upon a person's verbal expertise. There is growing evidence that large numbers of Americans are functionally illiterate, and a great number of Generation X-ers are much more visual than they are verbal. If you doubt this, browse through the advertising supplement of your Sunday newspaper and notice all the colorful, attention-grabbing ads for Nintendo, Sega, and other manufacturers of video games. Many of our kids are far more conversant with Super Mario and Sonic the Hedgehog than they are with Huckleberry Finn and Alice in Wonderland. This isolated fact is neither good nor bad—it's simply part of their culture. We must not make the mistake of confusing good readers with good disciples.

Since our children may well live their lives in a post-literate culture (and since many of them are more visually-oriented than word-oriented), we absolutely must rediscover how people learn values and beliefs in a non-print society. We, in fact, must rediscover the *imitatio* model. We should not give up our "study" model, but we must at least avoid forcing the model on others. Not everyone has been called to be a scribe, but everyone *has* been called to be a disciple of Jesus Christ. For this reason, parents and Christian educators must make the *imitatio* model the primary one in the home and in the local church.

Note the profoundly different emphases in the two models. The study or scribal approach emphasizes reason, textual prowess, and individual labor. The *imitatio* model emphasizes action, observation, modeling, and communal participation. The former elevates mind; the latter, heart and life.

TWO MODELS FOR ACHIEVING CHRISTLIKENESS

THE STUDY MODEL	*IMITATIO* MODEL
Reading	Observation
Words, Texts	Apprenticeship
Analysis	Action
Scribes	Disciples
Thinkers	People On A Journey
Isolation From Community	Immersion In Community

TABLE 9.1

While "study" flourishes in isolation, in the privacy of one's study or home, imitation presupposes a maturing process in an active, working fellowship. Our study of thousands of teens convinces us that spiritual formation must occur in the context of a loving, supportive community. This truth leads us to our last major point about imitation.

The Testimony of Mentors

Imitatio *is most fully realized when we model it for our young in a faith community.* Our research and our own years of experience as teachers, ministers, and parents, convince us that Christlikeness most often is achieved when young lives are continuously exposed to consistent examples of parents, teachers, and other spiritual guides. We have earlier asserted that spiritual formation is the gift of God, yet we must confess, in all wonder and humility, that God calls each one of us to be joint laborers with him in the process. Paul says in Ephesians that God "creates each of us by Jesus Christ to join him in the work he does, the good work . . . we had better be doing" (2:10, *The Message*). God works the miracle of transformation, but he typically uses teachers, parents, models, and mentors to effect the changes.

In a recent Lilly Endowment research project which focused on the reasons young people leave the Presbyterian Church, Dr. Benton Johnson and his colleagues concluded that the defections (which ran as high as 75%!) had little to do with the church's hierarchy or its theology. Rather, what was taught, discussed, and practiced *at the grass-roots level* (in the home and in the local congregation) determined whether members remained faithful to the denomination after they left home. The authors interviewed five hundred Presbyterian adults who had gone through confirmation. They asked, "Did you talk about religious matters in your homes? Did your parents bring up religious issues?" They found a direct relationship between the quality of conversation outside the church's walls and the durability of faith. They concluded: "To be effective, even the best conceived program of religious education needs the reinforcement of a rich, discursive follow-up in a circle of strong believers; two or three hours of God talk is hardly enough."[8] When religious values permeate a family's life, then children tend to remain in the church. Johnson argues that religious education has only minimal effect unless it is reinforced by discourse and example *outside* the church setting. For kids to absorb adult values, they need lots of incubation in a believing community where religion and values are openly talked about, not just silently assumed. Faith is contagious only if it is exercised openly, daily, sincerely.[9]

Not all spiritual modeling derives from living contemporaries or close friends or family. Consider Kim, a university student who in high school ceased to believe in God. A victim of family abuse as a child, she tried to numb her pain through sexual promiscuity and open rebellion against Christian values. Yet in college, Kim renewed her relationship with God through two dramatic cases of spiritual testimony.

First, she heard the personal testimony of a Christian professor who spoke frankly about his own faith struggles. Oddly, Kim did not hear the testimony firsthand, but indirectly through a friend. But the faith story was so authentic and compelling that it still affected her. Second, Kim says her life changed through her careful reading and contemplation of Augustine's *Confessions*. Kim was greatly moved by Augustine's sexual and spiritual struggles. She was particularly moved when she came to the passage which recounted the death of Monica, Augustine's mother, a woman who lived so faithfully with Augustine's father Patrick:

> Just like Augustine, I had been pleased by the Savior himself, but I was still reluctant to enter His narrowness. Then I read Augustine's words describing his mother: "She had no other husband either before or after [Patrick]." I felt as Augustine felt when, in my own eyes, I was stripped naked and my conscience cried out against me. So I made my decision to rededicate myself to God and never have sex again until I was married. I hope that this story and the stories of other saints will change [my boyfriend's] life as well.

Kim eventually left her boyfriend and made a permanent life change. In her case, a modern, living testimony and a very ancient one combined to change her outlook and behavior.

Apprenticeship Christianity

Unfortunately, today's secular models of education have caused us to think in excessively narrow terms. For many, education means the acquisition of truths, facts, and concepts. But discipleship implies discipline, a way of life, imitative behaviors, and a moral vision inspired by a personal leader. Disciples do more than read texts and take exams. Disciples walk and talk with the master, and their exams come every day as they meet the trials of ordinary life. Each day they are implicitly asked, "Can you be like Jesus, here and now, in this situation?" And they know the answer, though it's sometimes very hard to perform in the school of life. "I have set you an example that you should do as I have done for you" (John 13:15, NIV). Peter reiterates the final answer: "Christ suffered for you, leaving you an example, that you should follow in his steps" (1 Peter 2:21, NRSV).

Christians not only follow Jesus. They are also instructed to follow the examples of *others* who have imitated Christ well. Paul advised the Philippians, "Join together, my friends, in following my example. You have us for a model; imitate those whose way of life conforms to it" (3:17, Revised English Bible). The early Christians believed that one should search out models of Christlikeness, lives that incarnated the patience, love, and self-sacrifice of Jesus himself. Paul taught the churches to follow those who bear Christ's "signature," his wounds. In other words, they were instructed to follow Christians like Paul himself who "carry the marks of Jesus branded on my body" (Galatians 6:17, NRSV). Thus, *imitatio* places a crucial emphasis on the community in the shaping of faith. Modeling requires a rich array of mature models: "Treat younger men as brothers, older women as mothers, and younger women as sisters" (1 Timothy 5:1, NIV).

Younger Christians were taught to become apprentices to older ones and learn faith through shared experiences. And that is precisely the reason we find people like Eusebius of Caesarea, an influential historian of the ancient church, meticulously recording the lives of Christians in the early centuries of the church. Christian historians recorded the lives of "saints" in an attempt to preserve the stories of people who had imitated the life of Jesus, just as Paul had advised them.

Once we understand that early Christians absorbed biblical truths through story telling as well as through hearing Scripture read aloud in a living community, we gain a new understanding of "Bible study." Early disciples had a "pattern" theology, but the pattern was the life of Christ. They revered the Bible, not to achieve some legalistic mastery, but in order to meet the person of Jesus—their hero. Disciples were devoted to information about Jesus only as a means to a higher end—developing a Christlike spirit and character. And they honored their leaders, not because they had legal authority, but because these Spirit-filled lives were irresistible templates of Jesus Christ. Henri Nouwen writes in *The Road to Daybreak* of lives that are channels of the divine presence:

> God became flesh for us to show us that the way to come in touch with God's love is the human way, in which the limited and partial affection that people can give offers access to the unlimited and complete love of God, love that God has poured into the human heart.[10]

To the degree we have allowed ourselves to become vessels of the Holy Spirit and allowed God to reform us, we are Christ to one another. Frederick Buechner summarizes the goal of all spiritual formation: "The ultimate purpose of God is to make Christs of us."

If we take the *imitatio* model of the Bible seriously, it will reorder a great deal of our church and family lives. We will have to reconsider our concept of church leaders. The elders of the early church were preeminently the people who were doing the best job of modeling Jesus Christ. Rather than policy-makers, our leaders are to be spiritual guides, as the Hebrew writer explains: "Remember your leaders, who spoke the word of God to you. Consider the outcome of their way of life and imitate their faith" (13:7, NIV). Our children do not need corporate executives; they do need spiritual fathers and mothers. As Theodore of Studios asked in the eighth century, "What is more to be desired than a true father, a father-in-God?"[11] It's better to have one father in the gospel than 10,000 guardians, Paul says (1 Corinthians 4:14-17).

In the light of *imitatio* we should discover new (or rather ancient) meanings for the forms of community worship (such as baptism and the Lord's Supper) which are intended to shape us in the image of Christ. As we have argued in the chapter on baptism and family rituals, we learn through what we do with our bodies as well as what we think with our minds. Corporate forms of worship were designed to teach and proclaim the life of Jesus as it is dramatized in our lives.

Imitatio also will prevent us from defining faith individualistically—the believer alone with his Lord—for in the imitation model our Lord is always incarnate in his living church. He has never left us. He is seen in the Christians around us, in the martyrs, in the clouds of witnesses about us, both living and dead. One of the Desert Fathers said this: "If you see a young man climbing up to heaven by his own will, seize him by the foot and pull him down, for this is to his own profit."[12] The expression is bold, but the idea is pure Gospel: you cannot make it alone; you need your brothers and sisters.

Generation X-ers have great difficulty understanding the theological disputes of the past, but they will respond to the Gospel story. They know intuitively that the shortest distance between truth and the human heart is a story. *Imitatio* spirituality, which relies heavily on narrative and story telling, can lead them to a revitalized theology. Abstract language about God, often imported from Greek philosophy, makes very little sense to them. But they will respond to the simple stories from the life of Jesus, stories from believers who are embodiments of the One Story. Imitation of Christ will communicate in a way that scholasticism cannot.

Imitatio *and Human Suffering*

Imitatio offers another benefit to our children: It can help them understand the role of suffering in their lives. As we completed our previous book, *Dying To Tell*, it occurred to us that young people have great trouble accepting suffering because they live in a culture that denies the meaning and purpose of suffering. In a hedonistic culture such as ours, suffering is a scandal, a sign of failure. Many of our children have no theology of suffering. However, the story of Jesus is centrally concerned with suffering. Jesus gives meaning to pain.

Why is so much of the Gospel devoted to one week in the life of Jesus? Why does the Passion narrative occupy half of John's Gospel? The story of imitation asks disciples to identify with Jesus in his sorrows, to take up the cross and struggle. Scripture assumes that Jesus' followers can and will imitate him in his sufferings: "As he is so are we in the world" (1 John 4:17, NRSV). "We are children and heirs," Paul affirms, "if we suffer with Christ" (Romans 8:17, NRSV). "I want to know Christ and the power of his resurrection and the sharing of his sufferings by becoming like him in his death. . ." (Philippians 3:10, NRSV).

Imitatio naturally leads to the spiritual disciplines. It is not accidental that the literature of spirituality clearly emphasizes both the spiritual disciplines and imitation since they function reciprocally. The disciplines inspire imitation; imitation leads one back to the disciplines. By separating the believer, however briefly, from the seductions of daily life, the disciplines free one to focus on how Christ spoke, behaved, and touched people. The disciplines empower one to follow Jesus' example. The disciplines bring us face to face with Jesus. When one comes face to face with Jesus, he cannot help looking and acting like him. "We shall be like him, for we shall see him as he is," John tells us (1 John 3:2, NIV). Helen H. Lemmel expresses it eloquently in her 1922 hymn:

> Turn your eyes upon Jesus,
> Look full in his wonderful face,
> And the things of earth will grow strangely dim
> In the light of his glory and grace.

Imitatio *and Outreach*

Finally, *imitatio* inevitably leads to evangelism. More exactly, imitating Jesus *is* evangelism in its purest form. Evangelism without imitation is hypocrisy. Imitation without evangelism is inconceivable. How could one be like Jesus without attracting notice? "Performing" the life of Jesus in humility, self-sacrifice, and compassion is inevitably arresting. Paul believes in the connection between proclamation and imitation: "We proclaim Jesus Christ as Lord and ourselves as your slaves for Jesus' sake" (2 Corinthians 4:5, NRSV). When we carry in our bodies the death of Jesus, it always follows that the life of Jesus is made visible (2 Corinthians 4:10-11). The great Renaissance preacher and poet, George Herbert, once described the mysterious connection between the evangelist's life and the message that he carries to the world. While we may separate message and life for purposes of discussion, the people of the world only see one thing, either the representation of the gospel or a lie. Herbert writes in "The Windows":

Lord, how can man preach thy eternal word?
He is a brittle crazy glass:
Yet in thy temple thou dost him afford
This glorious and transcendent place,
To be a window, through thy grace.
But when thou dost anneal in glass thy story,
Making thy life to shine within
The holy preacher's; then the light and glory
More rev'rend grows, and more doth win:
Which else shows wat'rish, bleak, and thin.
Doctrine and life, colours and light, in one
When they combine and mingle, bring
A strong regard and awe: but speech alone
Doth vanish like a flaring thing,
And in the ear, not conscience ring.

Either our lives are bright with the light of Jesus or they are not. If we practice *imitatio*, we are windows of grace, and the story is "annealed"—burned and impressed upon us. Our beliefs and our lives are not two things, finally, but one. When the One Life of Christ is folded into our own, his brightness shoots through us like sunlight through stained glass.

So also, when our children imitate their Savior, they will be spiritually mature, and the world will know Jesus.

---

[1] For an excellent study of the biblical roots of *imitatio Christi* see E. J. Tinsley, *The Imitation of God in Christ* (Philadelphia: Westminster Press, 1960).

[2] C. S. Lewis, *The Problem of Pain* (New York: Macmillan, 1962) 104.

[3] See Allan H. Sager, *Gospel-Centered Spirituality: An Introduction to Our Spiritual Journey* (Minneapolis: Augsburg, 1990).

[4] Qtd. in Otto Gründler, "Devotio Moderna" in *Christian Spirituality: High Middle Ages and Reformation* Ed. Jill Raitt (New York: Crossroad, 1988) 190.

[5] See Otto Gründler, 190-191. While we dispute the "either/or" approach in Gründler's essay, we can appreciate his calling our attention to the Reformation's casting aside of meditative readings as it turned to more analytical ones. We may ask, though, "Why can't we benefit from both explication and meditation, while admitting the limitations of either in isolation?"

[6] See Walter Ong, "The Orality of the Mindset in the Biblical Texts is Overwhelming," *Orality and Literacy: The Technologizing of the Word* (New York: Methuen, 1982) 74.

[7] Augustine, *Confessions* VI.3 (Oxford: UP, 1991) 92-93.

[8] Benton Johnson et al., "Mainline Churches: The Real Reason for Decline" *First Things* (March 1993): 16ff.

[9] See our discussion of parental spiritual leadership in Chapter Five.

[10] Henri Nouwen, *The Road to Daybreak: A Spiritual Journey* (New York: Doubleday/Image, 1990) 59-60.

[11] Qtd. in Kallistos Ware, "Ways of Prayer and Contemplation" in *Christian Spirituality: Origins to the Twelfth Century* Ed. Bernard McGinn et al. (New York: Crossroad, 1987) 407. Theodore of Studios was an eighth-century Byzantine theologian.

[12] Qtd. in Ware, 407. The Desert Fathers were a group of distinguished monastics who retreated to the Egyptian desert in the fourth century A.D. For more information, see Henri Nouwen, *Way of the Heart,* or Helen Waddell, *The Desert Fathers.*

10
A Plan For Building Adolescent Spirituality

Seek me with all your heart and you will be found by me.
—Jeremiah 29:13

Spirituality is not the latest fad but the oldest truth. Spirituality, the alert attention we give to a living God and the faithful response we make to him in community, is the heart of our Scriptures and is on display throughout the centuries of Israel and the church. —Eugene Peterson

Tell me the story of Jesus. Write on my heart every word.
—Fanny J. Crosby

When we began this project, one of our most difficult tasks was to define "spirituality." For some, like Joseph Sittler, spirituality is "the power, presence, dynamics of the Spirit," and, by its very nature, "not a definable reality." To Ernest Boyer, Jr., spirituality is "anything that reveals how close God is to us." For Thomas Merton it's the contemplative side to faith. To Eugene Peterson it is "the alert attention we give to a living God and the faithful response we make to him in community." This latter definition approaches our own. At its core, spirituality is simply *knowing and loving God.* Of course, one cannot scientifically measure knowing and loving God. But we can measure what people tell us about their experience of knowing and loving God, and that has been our goal.

Evidence of a spiritual life came from the answers we received to three basic questions:

1. Do our adolescents take God seriously?
2. Does Christ make a difference in their lives?
3. Do our teens report an experience with the Holy Spirit?

These three critical issues compose what researchers call the "dependent variables." (See the box placed at the right in Figure 10.1) As researchers, we were interested in what explains the box on the right—adolescent spirituality (the dependent variables). To solve this problem, our research design called for a regression analysis in which hundreds of "independent variables" were regressed onto the dependent variable. The result is the predictive model shown in Figure 10.1. This empirical model helps us answer some fundamental questions: What causes kids to take God seriously? What encourages them to allow Christ to be their ultimate decision maker? What separates kids who are serious about the Holy Spirit and his influence in their lives from those who aren't?

We have described the statistical data in this book as "correlational data." By correlational data we are talking about associations, relationships, or linkages between (or among) two or more variables. For example, we know from our research that as positive family communication increases, teens are more likely to take God seriously, let Christ make a difference in their lives, and report the indwelling of the Holy Spirit. However, it is important to state that a correlation does not necessarily imply a cause-and-effect relationship. For example, in the case of family communication described above, it may be the case that teens who are more spiritual influence family communication in a positive manner. Or conversely, family communication could be the positive influence on teen spirituality. One can never know a cause with scientific certainty when dealing with correlations. However, when enough correlations are established, the vectors of evidence coalesce and point toward reasonable conclusions. In view of the overwhelming consistency in the correlations we have established, therefore, we can describe a predictive model.

We believe our predictive model (Figure 10.1) has significant implications both for ministry and family life. This model is based on consistent findings from three years of research, combined with findings from previous studies in the research literature. Finally, we have used a predictive statistical tool called "multiple-regression" analysis. Multiple regression uses all of the potential variables and produces a ranking or weight for each one, according to its role in explaining adolescent spirituality.

Looking at the left column in Figure 10.1, one sees ten variables which predict adolescent spirituality. That is to say, if the positive variables in this list (those marked with a + sign) are present in a teenager's life, he or she will much more likely take God seriously. If a teen has one of the negative variables in his life, he or she will take God less seriously. We assert, then, that these are the ten most critical issues for ministry to teens and their families. These top ten factors can actually be said to cause, influence, and even predict positive outcomes in the area of adolescent spirituality.

A MODEL FOR ADOLESCENT SPIRITUALITY

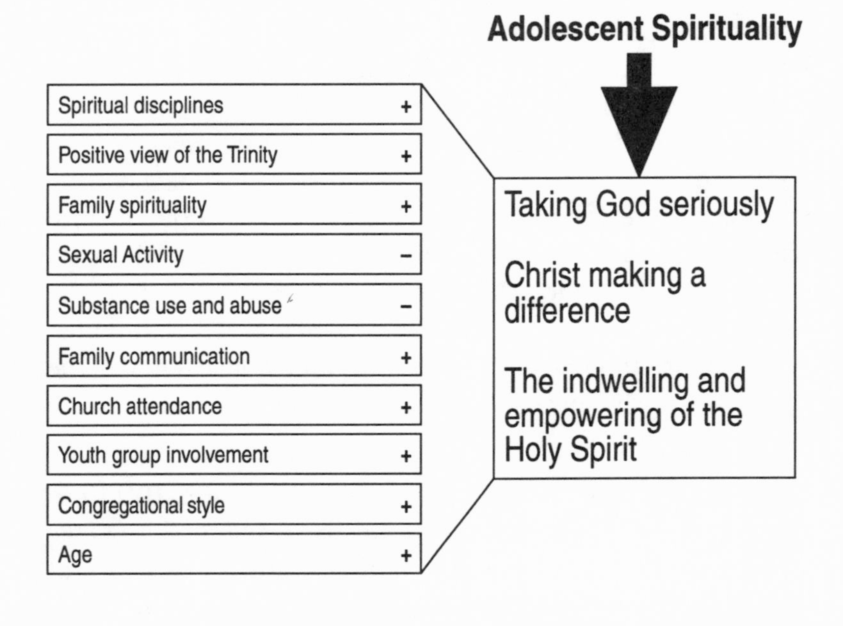

FIGURE 10.1

1st Predictor: The Practice of the Spiritual Disciplines

To our surprise, the consistent practice of the spiritual disciplines proved to be the most important predictor for adolescent spirituality. The greater the use of the spiritual disciplines and the more intense their use, the more likely teens are to take God seriously, to allow Christ to make a difference in their lives, and to feel empowered by the Holy Spirit. Some of the spiritual disciplines included in our study were meditative prayer, daily reading of the Bible, confession, weeping over the lost, praise or celebration, and fasting.

2nd Predictor: A Positive View of God

Adolescents who feel positively about God take him more seriously. Thus, our ability to present God in a way that makes sense to our teens and encourages them is the second most critical task for those ministering to young people. It is urgent that we understand the heart cries of Generation X and those aspects of God's nature that might attract or compel them.

3rd Predictor: Family Spirituality

Throughout this book we have emphasized the importance of parental modeling of the faith walk. The point is not primarily that adults need to convince kids they need God. Rather, parents need to demonstrate this truth personally through their consistent, faithful examples.

4th Predictor: Sexual Involvement

Sexual activity is the first *negative* predictor of adolescent spirituality. Teens who are sexually active are simply less likely to take God seriously, allow Christ to make a difference or to feel empowered by the Holy Spirit. Conversely, those who keep themselves sexually pure are more likely to be spiritually oriented.

5th Predictor: Substance Abuse

Substance abuse proves to be another *negative* predictor of adolescent spirituality. As we found in our previous studies on adolescent morality, teens who choose to use and abuse chemical substances are at great spiritual risk. The use of drugs and alcohol distracts to such a degree that it makes the spiritual life very difficult to appreciate. It is not surprising that Paul casts chemical abuse in an adversarial role with the life of the Spirit: "Do not get drunk with wine, for that is debauchery, but be filled with the Spirit" (Ephesians 5:18, NRSV).

6th Predictor: Family Communication

Interactional patterns within the family system are another powerful predictor of adolescent spirituality. This variable concerns the parents' ability to listen, to be available, to be open, and to value the thoughts and opinions of their teens. When parents doubt they can have much influence, when they doubt they have anything to contribute to their children's spiritual heath, we remind them of this point: providing open space for fearless communication is a priceless spiritual gift which will bless their children's lives.

7th Predictor: Church Attendance

Willingness to be involved in the life of the congregation is another predictor of spirituality. It is unfortunate when teens are separated from the worship experiences of the larger body, since spiritual maturity requires contact and communion with the full body of Christ. Too often teens are isolated in their daily lives from adults. Often parents are absent from the home. Teens are often "age-segregated" at school and even at their jobs. Our children desperately need to see spiritually mature people at work and at worship. We should remember, though, that the degree to which the congregation positively impacts our children is partly dependent upon the congregation's style. (See the 9th predictor, below).

8th Predictor: Youth Group Activities

Involvement in a youth ministry program is another important key to the spiritual life. Our teens need to be around peers who will encourage them to grow to be like Jesus. Like all believers, our teens need to experience the approval, understanding, and discipline of caring friends. In the words of Dietrich Bonhoeffer, they need "love with skin on it." Friends in the youth program provide one of the best ways to receive the encouragement to live a godly, Christ-focused life.

9th Predictor: Congregational Style

An adolescent's perception of the church system is critical to teen spirituality. By "church system" we mean congregational personality, complexion, or ambiance. Is the local church affirming, relevant, sensitive—or cold, rigid, and unforgiving? If a teenager views the local church as positive and encouraging, then she is definitely encouraged in her spiritual life. Here is another area where parents and church leaders have an important contribution to make to adolescent faith-building. If parents choose a positive congregation and if church leaders intentionally build a positive congregational style, then our children will more likely grow into spiritually mature adults.

10th Predictor: Age

All of our surveys of adolescents since we began our empirical research in 1988 have revealed the same fundamental truth: *spiritual formation is age-related.* In particular, our studies indicate that there are two watershed years for our teens: ages 16 and 18. Of course, age 16 marks the time at which most children get their driver's licenses. Many receive their own automobiles and achieve a large measure of freedom from Mom and Dad. Age 18, the year of high school graduation for most adolescents, signals an additional stage of independence from parents. For many, this age signals the exit from the family dwelling and a dramatic new orientation in life—toward new friends, new interests, and new goals, including college or career in another locale. These ages indicate "emancipation" from home—a necessary and desirable goal if our children are to become autonomous adults. Yet these times of increased freedom are also occasions when faith and values are severely tested. Parents should be particularly alert to changes in behavior and attitude as their children are emancipated.

The Children of Our Tears

Responsible parents and church leaders should be acutely aware of the ten predictors of spirituality. If we encourage the presence of the eight positive predictors, we can be confident we are doing our best to assist our children to develop their own personal faith. Yet we must repeat what we said in the preface to this book. There are no guarantees in child-rearing. "Train up a child in the way he should go: and when he is old, he will not depart from it" (Proverbs 22:6, NRSV) is one of the most misused Scriptures in Christendom. Too often this aphorism has been used as a stick to beat depressed and disheartened parents.

It is time to declare the obvious: a proverb is, *by definition*, a "generalization," a "truism," to which there can be many exceptions. We have always recognized this point when considering other proverbs, but for some reason, people apply Proverbs 22:6 in a universal way quite inappropriate to the text. All one has to do is read the rest of Proverbs 22 and ask the question: do any of the other proverbs in this chapter have exceptions? It turns out, many of them do. Consider, for example, verse 11: "Those who love a pure heart and are gracious in speech will have the king as a friend" (NRSV). Can this proverb be *universally* true? If it were, then one would never find a case in which a pure, gracious person ever came into conflict with a ruler. This is, of course, patently absurd. Jesus, Paul, and Peter frequently came into conflict with kings. Surely, this doesn't mean that Jesus, Paul, or Peter lacked a pure heart or gracious speech!? No, it just means that the Proverbs writer is writing a "proverb". Generally speaking, you get along with the authorities better if you are pure and gracious of speech. Similarly, Proverbs 22:6 is asserting a truism: good child-rearing practices generally pay off. But certainly, there are exceptions.

We say all this to remind our readers that child-rearing is complicated and arduous. Of course, parents should do their best, and most do. But doing our level best will not guarantee that our children will have the faith we want them to have. The time comes to trust, to pray, and to hope—like the good father in Luke 15.

One of our favorite stories about patient parenting comes from the life of Augustine. In his youth, Augustine's mother Monica was deeply distressed that her son was following the life of a pagan unbeliever. Monica, a devoted Christian, went to a shepherd of the church and begged him to intervene and somehow manipulate her son into the kingdom of God. But the wise shepherd refused. He told Monica, "only pray the Lord for him." But Monica would not give in.

> She pressed him with more begging and with floods of tears, asking him to see [Augustine] and debate with [him]. [The bishop] was now irritated and a little vexed and said: "Go away from me: as you live, it cannot be that the son of these tears should perish."[1]

Augustine did return to God, but only after many years of rebellion. In her conversations with her son after his conversion, Monica recalled that "she had taken these words [from the shepherd] as if they had sounded from heaven." To all the parents who have done all they know to do, to all those who have prayed and wept, we offer the same advice that

Monica heard, "As you live, it cannot be that the child of these tears should perish." We must trust—even when we cannot see.

Practical Suggestions

There are a great many practical ways adults can help their children grow up in God. We have made many suggestions throughout this book, but as we close we wish to restate a few steps parents, youth ministers, and church leaders could initiate.

1. *Get thoroughly acquainted with Generation X.* Many books and articles are available on the subject. Here are a few for starters:

   Barna, George. *The Invisible Generation: Baby Busters.* Glendale, CA: Barna Research Group, 1992.

   Coupland, Douglas. *Generation X: Tales for an Accelerated Culture.* New York: St. Martin's, 1991.

   —. *Life After God.* New York: Simon & Schuster, 1994.

   Gibb, Steven. *Twentysomething, Floundering, and Off the Yuppie Track.* Chicago: Noble Press, 1992.

   Mahedy, William and Janet Bernardi. *A Generation Alone: Xers Making a Place in the World.* Downers Grove: InterVarsity, 1994.

   Strauss, William and Neil Howe. *Generations: The History of America's Future.* New York: William Morrow, 1990.

   —. *Thirteenth Gen: Abort, Retry, Ignore, Fail?* New York: Random House, 1993.

2. *Form a study group at church or in your home to educate parents and other concerned adults about the culture of our children.* Build a network of caring adults who will support each other as you minister to youths.

3. *Pray faithfully for your children and your children's friends and peers.* In your prayer time, specifically ask God to deliver you from your fears. Pray the Psalms and apply the wisdom of the Psalms to your daily, family situations.

4. *Engage your children frequently in conversation about matters of faith and ethics.* Communicate, communicate, communicate! This includes granting permission to your children to question, debate, and challenge. Remember the wise words of the greatest preacher of the seventeenth century, John Donne: "Doubt wisely; in strange way/To stand inquiring, is not to stray." Select some of the topics from this book and make them the topic of an evening's family discussion. For example:

    - Talk with your children about "core" beliefs. What belongs to the core and what does not? Listen and share your belief about the fundamentals. Grant them permission to do the same.

    - After thoroughly familiarizing yourself with "Generation X" thinking, select a few ideas and discuss them with your children. Don't be surprised if your children reject many of the generalizations about Gen X. Most teens are not "cynical, purple-haired blob[s] watching TV" though their critics portray them that way.[2] X-ers, like most people, hate labeling and stereotyping. Ask them to talk about the problem.

- Ask your kids to critique you and your generation. Using the scale from Chapter Four (p. 84) which lists the qualities kids admire most in parents, ask your kids to tell you how you are doing. This is one time to practice supernatural patience and forbearance. Don't defend or explain. Just listen and reflect.
- Tell your children the story of your own spiritual pilgrimage. Have you told them why you became a Christian? When, where, how? Do they know the story of your own struggles to serve God? Do they know how God has changed your life? If they haven't heard these things, it's time. In return, ask them to tell the story of their efforts to know God.

5. *Evaluate yourself.* In particular, determine how much time you spend with your children. Many parents assume that they spend more time with their kids than they really do. Honestly assess how much focused attention you've given your children in the last month. If it's less than a half hour a day on average, reconsider your priorities.
6. *Get serious about practicing the spiritual disciplines in your family life.* Some authorities say that it takes three years to make a behavior a life-long habit or practice. Become familiar with the spiritual disciplines through good reading, and then adapt the disciplines to your particular family's needs.[3]
7. *Support and strengthen the youth and family ministry program in your congregation.* Year after year, the ACU Center for Adolescent Studies reaffirms the importance of youth and family

ministry programs. Youth ministers are often second only to parents in terms of spiritual impact on teens. Make it easy for your child to be an active participant in the congregation's youth program. Avoid allowing school activities to override youth program events. Every church needs a strong, vibrant outreach to teens. Build one and support it.

8. *Ask the youth leaders in your congregation to plan plenty of service, missions, and worship activities.* Compare last year's youth calendar at your church with the youth activities in Chapter Four. How many of these recommended programs are available in your church? If the answer is, "not many," offer to sponsor the programs that teens tell us really help them. You don't have to wait on a church to sponsor them, either. On your own or with other families, you can see to it that your children have opportunities to attend camps and go on mission trips.

9. *Start a mentoring or apprenticeship program in your congregation.* End the age segregation that harms spiritual formation by sponsoring intergenerational activities for your children. Learn from the scouting programs in your area—plan activities in which mature spiritual adults will come to know, work beside, and recreate with your children. In turn, make yourself available to children in your congregation besides your own. Become a mentor, in other words, to two or three children in your local church. Invite adult Christians to share their own testimonies about how God has called them to their particular vocations. Form a committee to come up with

other ways to implement "apprenticeship" Christianity in your congregation.

10. *Introduce your children to their spiritual heritage.* Never denigrate your spiritual tradition. Instead, introduce your children to its richness, variety, and meaning. Teach them the good in tradition, even while pointing out its dangers. Establish your own family traditions and make them a central aspect of your family life. Teach (and practice) a deep respect for the forms and rites of worship.

11. *Establish a study group at your congregation to consider the role of faith-building rituals in the community of faith.* Consider new ways to give visual, dramatic emphasis to the forms of faith such as baptism .[4] When the time comes for your child to be baptized, make it a major occasion. Give it enough attention and prominence so your child will never forget the importance of his or her decision.

12. *Trust in God and forgive yourself.* Most of our suggestions are preventative measures. However, some of our readers have children who have already gravitated beyond the home environment. Some of our children have already made crucial decisions that have already, or soon will, separate them from the faith community. What can you do if your child has already, more or less, exited from the culture of belief? First, we must go on trusting. The stories from Scripture and our own personal experience teach us to be people of hope. We must trust that our children have memories of faith, that like the wayward son in Luke 15, they will someday remember that home is better than the hog pen. We must also keep reaching out to them

in love, resisting the temptation to burn the bridges. We must imitate the steadfast love and patience of our Father who maintains high standards but who never, never gives up on us. Finally, we must confess our failures, accept God's forgiveness, and forgive ourselves. Every parent can always say, "I could have done better." But it's also true that there is grace for imperfect parents. We must learn to forgive ourselves, knowing that God loves us in our failure, just as he loves our children in theirs. Here is perhaps our finest opportunity to grow up in love—bearing all things, believing all things, hoping all things, enduring all things. "Love never ends."

"This Is for Keeps"

We conclude by returning to the central question behind this book: "Will our children know God?" So much depends upon God. So much depends upon us. We may not be miracle workers, but we can create a culture where belief is a vibrant option. We cannot do the impossible, but we can be sensible, committed, and thoroughly equipped for the battles that lie ahead. As *The Message* puts it:

> God is strong, and he wants you strong. Please take everything the Master has set out for you, well-made weapons of the best materials. And put them to use so you will be able to stand up to everything the Devil throws your way. This is no afternoon athletic contest that we'll walk away from and forget about in a couple of hours. This is for keeps, a life-or-death fight to the finish against the Devil and all his angels. (Ephesians 6:10-12)

---

[1] Augustine, *Confessions* Book III.12, Trans. Henry Chadwick (Oxford: UP, 1991): 51.

[2] Jeff Giles, "Generalizations X" *Newsweek* 6 June 1994: 63.

[3] For a full bibliography on the spiritual disciplines send a self-addressed stamped envelope to the Center for Adolescent Studies, ACU Box 8451, Abilene, TX 79699. In addition, we recommend Richard Foster, *The Celebration of Discipline* (San Francisco: Harper and Row, 1988), and *Prayer: Finding the Heart's True Home* (San Francisco: HarperSanFrancisco, 1992); Dallas Willard, *The Spirit of the Disciplines* (San Francisco: Harper and Row, 1988); Henri Nouwen, *Reaching Out: The Three Movements of the Spiritual Life* (Garden City: Doubleday, 1975), and *The Way of the Heart: Desert Spirituality and Contemporary Ministry* (Cambridge: Harper and Row, 1981).

[4] We recommend that church leaders, parents, and ministers consider a recent unpublished study of how congregations can instill faith into children who are approaching the age of decision-making about baptism. See Tommy W. King, "Faith Decisions: Christian Initiation for the Children of the Glenwood Church of Christ." D. Min. Project Thesis, Abilene Christian University, 1994.

INDEX TO FIGURES & TABLES

A

C

D

G

H

I

L

M

P

Q

R

S

T

W

Y